No. 5

Brief Lives

RUPERT OF THE RHINE

Brief Lives

PRINCE RUPERT OF THE RHINE BY LELY
Reproduced by gracious permission of H.M. The Queen

RUPERT
of the
RHINE

By

BERNARD FERGUSSON

BRIEF LIVES

COLLINS, ST JAMES'S PLACE

LONDON

FOR LAURA

PRINTED IN GREAT BRITAIN
COLLINS CLEAR-TYPE PRESS: LONDON AND GLASGOW
1952

FOREWORD

THE period of the Civil War abounds in absorbing characters; but none is more attractive than Prince Rupert—Rupert of the Rhine. He owed his nickname to the small state of the Palatinate, some way up the Rhine Valley, from which he sprang, although, oddly enough, he never saw it until after the end of the war with which his name his chiefly associated. His character was by no means without blemish, and he was sometimes technically at fault; but he was often brilliant, and his stout heart never failed, whether ashore or afloat, in battle or in the hunting-field. There is a rough consistency about him throughout his life, from the days when he was an impetuous youth until he was a bluff old man in London and Windsor, when even King Charles II was a trifle scared of him. I have caught myself thinking more than once how much he would have revelled in some of the more enterprising ventures of the late war—the Long Range Desert Group, the Special Air Service, the Special Boat Section, the Chindits, or with partisans in occupied Europe. As a professional soldier whose hobbies are sailing and travel, I find I love him very much.

This book will be found to adhere closely to his own fortunes. The causes of the Civil War, its prosecution in Scotland and Ireland, the state of England under the Commonwealth are scarcely mentioned at all. It is difficult enough to confine Rupert within the covers of a short book; if one were to take one's eye off him even for a moment, he would slip away as surely as he did from Kinsale and the Tagus.

I am most grateful to all who have helped me, especially to Mr. Robert Birley, Mr. C. R. N. Routh and Mr. T. F. Cattley, who are respectively Headmaster, Senior History Master and School Librarian of Eton, and all of whom taught me there; to Sir Owen Morshead and Miss Mackenzie, of Her Majesty's Library at Windsor Castle; to Colonel Shepperd, of the Central Library of the Royal Military Academy, Sandhurst; to Lord Russell of Liverpool, for enabling me to visit Vlotho and for obtaining local accounts of the battle there; to Miss C. V. Wedgwood; and to Commander G. J. Kirkby, D.S.C., R.N., a present colleague, for checking nautical detail. But I am most deeply in the debt of a man who died a hundred years ago. Eliot Warburton's three-volume *Memoirs of Prince Rupert and the Cavaliers* (London, 1849) blazed the trail which all must follow. His industry was prodigious; he had none of the aids, such as the publications of the Historical Manuscripts Commission or the Navy Records Society, which his successors enjoy; and he produced an eminently readable and reliable book, including many letters and most of the Prince's Diaries. He perished at sea at the age of forty-two, three years after his book appeared.

CONTENTS

LIST OF MAPS

* 1 *

Seed-Time

O<small>N THE</small> 14th of February 1613 a young couple was married in the Chapel of Whitehall, in London. Neither of the two was yet seventeen. The bridegroom was Frederick, the Elector Palatine; the bride was Elizabeth, daughter of King James the First. Frederick, who had come to England four months before the wedding, was a serious-minded and gloomy youth; Elizabeth was impetuous, rather selfish, spoilt and exceedingly beautiful. It was said to be a love-match, but there were weighty diplomatic reasons for the marriage: the Elector was one of the not very numerous Calvinist princes on the Continent, and the King was a leading champion of the Protestant cause.

The wedding was a splendid occasion. So gorgeous were the bridegroom's presents to the bride—among them " two pearls esteemed the rarest in Christendom " —that the King forbade him to give her any more. Prince Charles, the future Charles the First, escorted his sister to the Chapel, and the King gave her away. For the next two nights London gave itself up to masques and rejoicings; there was to be an even greater entertainment on the third night, but the crowds were so enormous that it had to be cancelled.

A week later, escorted by four English lords, the couple disembarked at Flushing in Holland, and journeyed to Heidelberg, Frederick's capital, 350 miles up the Rhine. And there they might have lived long and happily, if it had not been for Elizabeth's ambition. The people of Heidelberg had taken her to their heart, calling her " The Pearl of Britain," but after the glories of the English Court Heidelberg seemed to her provincial. In 1619 the throne of Bohemia fell vacant. The Holy Roman Emperor nominated his cousin Ferdinand, a faithful Catholic, to the succession; but the Bohemian nobles were mostly Calvinists and wished for a Calvinist king; they ejected the Emperor's emissaries from a window—the Defenestration of Prague—and offered the crown to Frederick. He hesitated, but Elizabeth was determined to be a Queen rather than a mere Electress. " You were bold enough to marry the daughter of a king," she said, " and you hesitate to accept a crown? I would rather live on bread with a King than feast with an Elector! " Years later she repented of her advice: but Frederick was persuaded, and on the 4th of November 1619 they were crowned King and Queen in Prague.

The Emperor was furious, but he bided his time, while Frederick and Elizabeth enjoyed for the moment the gaieties of Prague; they were to be known to history as the Winter King and Queen, because their reign lasted barely a year. When they arrived in Prague they already had two sons and a daughter; within a few weeks their third son was born to them; and this was Rupert. His christening was marked by a splendour reminiscent of his parents' marriage. Of all their twelve children, he was the only one born to them while they were King and Queen, and not merely Elector and Electress or homeless exiles. The whole of Prague rejoiced; and the royal baby was handed in turn from noble sponsor to noble sponsor. Splendid presents were showered on him; and among them was a silver ship, prophetic of years which were not the least glorious of the life which he was destined to lead.

But a few weeks after this christening, and one year and two weeks after the coronation, the Bohemian army was defeated in a single battle outside Prague, and the royal family was in flight. They fled so quickly that Rupert was nearly left behind: a courtier heard him crying, snatched him up and thrust him into the last carriage. It was bitter weather with snow on the ground; at one stage the Queen had to leave her coach and ride pillion behind young Ralph Hopton, an English gentleman of her court, whose destiny was to be woven into that of Rupert. They did not dare pause in their flight until Brandenburg, nearly 200 miles from Prague, where the Elector was a relation of Frederick's. He was fearful of the Emperor and unwilling to give them asylum, but the Queen was about to have another child, and he allowed them to wait for her confinement. In these unpropitious conditions was born Maurice, who was destined to be Rupert's favourite brother and fellow rover, and to share many of his adventures ashore and afloat.

As soon as the Queen could travel the fugitives set off again. Heidelberg was closed to them: in gambling for a kingdom Frederick had lost his electorate as well. Henceforward he and his family were to be exiles. They found refuge in Holland with the Prince of Orange, Frederick's uncle; and the other children, who had been separated from their parents during the flight, gathered round them at The Hague. A house was found at Leyden, twelve miles out from the capital; but Elizabeth took little interest in her children until they were old enough to amuse her: she made the Leyden house into a nursery, while she and Frederick lived in the livelier society of The Hague. He was persistently unhappy and hated his surroundings: she, though chafing at the loss of both Bohemia and the Palatinate, had plenty to console her. English men of fashion travelled to The Hague to pay court to her beauty; some, like Sir Thomas Roe and Lord Craven, joined her family circle and served her with devotion of many years; and Sir Henry Wotton, who was shortly to become Provost of Eton, began a long correspondence with her, in the course of which he made light of the not inconsiderable distance between Eton and The Hague. It was he who, in the exquisite verses *To His Mistress, the Queen of Bohemia*, compared her in the space of fifteen lines to the Moon, the Nightingale and the Rose.

Meanwhile at Leyden the family was growing and being educated. For all that they were without a kingdom, they were not allowed to forget that they were royal; the little princes and princesses were taught to treat each other with enormous ceremony, and to observe all the graces of a genuine court. Rupert was impatient with much of what he had to learn, but he excelled at such subjects as took his fancy. Leyden was a University town, thronged with scholars, painters and writers; and Rupert acquired a good knowledge of languages and a taste for drawing and painting. At the same time he developed a voracious appetite for the joys of the open air. He shot, he hunted, he rode, he swam, and he learned to play tennis, a sport at which, years afterwards, when he was an elderly man, he was accounted by Pepys to be one of the four best players in England. His elder brothers, Henry and Charles-Louis, were staid and serious like their father: so was his sister Elizabeth, who was afterwards to become Abbess of a Protestant sister-hood. Even in those earliest days Maurice was his companion. There was a streak of mischief in both of them, but Rupert, growing taller and handsome and very strong, was always the leader: his sisters called him "Rupert-le-Diable," and his high spirits worried his mother. She, indeed, never wholly approved of him throughout his life; and as he grew older she was con-stantly asking Sir Thomas Roe to talk to him like a father. Lord Craven had no influence over Rupert at all; the young princes used to laugh at Craven, and call him "the little mad milord"; he was the rich son of a self-made father, and perhaps the Princes, conscious of their splendid lineage, looked down upon his parentage: but Rupert had cause to be grateful to him before long.

The King of England and the Prince of Orange both died in 1625, but their successors, who were respectively Elizabeth's brother and Frederick's cousin, continued to support the exiles, whom ill-luck still pursued. Dutch generosity had given them a share in a fleet of ships trading to the Far East; and one day in 1629 came the news that this convoy, on which their hopes were set, was approaching the coast of Holland. Frederick and his eldest son Henry travelled to Amsterdam to meet it. They were going down river in a small boat to watch the ships coming in when their craft was run down and sunk by a bigger vessel, and the boy was drowned. From that moment, heavy with grief, Frederick grew more and more morose. Three years later he joined Gustavus Adolphus of Sweden, who, during a campaign against the Empire, had actually recovered part of the Palatinate; but Frederick died of a fever, Gustavus Adolphu was killed in a skirmish, and the war petered out, leaving the Palatinate complete in the Emperor's hands.

The future of the family was now poor indeed; they had lost their father, their brother, their prospects of a fortune, and their hopes of recovering their home. The four eldest boys wrote an affecting letter to Charles the First:

> We commit ourselves and the protection of our rights into your gracious arms, humbly beseeching your Majesty so to look upon us as upon those who have neither friends nor fortune nor greater honour in this world than belongs to your royal blood. Unless you please to maintain that in us, God knoweth what may become of your Majesty's nephews.

CHARLES   RUPERT   MAURICE   EDWARD

As a result of this letter, signed by four boys of whom

the eldest was only twelve, King Charles invited his
sister to make her home in England; but she refused,
perhaps to his relief. He helped her with money so far
as he could, but he himself was in distress for lack of it.
It seemed that the only hope for the boys was to become
soldiers of fortune, and a chance offered a few years later.
The new Prince of Orange was planning a campaign
against the town of Rheinberg, twenty miles beyond his
frontier on the left bank of the Rhine; and Charles-Louis
and Rupert, aged fifteen and thirteen, went with him.
The life was vastly to the taste of Rupert who was
already a young giant, and he made an excellent impression on the Prince's officers. Back at The Hague,
when the short campaign was over, Dutch society made
much of him, and he showed signs of being a great deal
too big for his boots; so his mother packed him off,
back to his books at Leyden. Two years later he went
to the wars again with the Prince's forces, and took part
in three engagements; this time he not only conducted
himself well, but showed a knowledge of the theory of
war, which he had been studying in the years between.

While Rupert was in the field, Charles-Louis, now
eighteen, was making his first visit to England. He was
a personable young man, well-mannered and grave, and
his fond mother was gratified to get good reports of him
from King Charles, Sir Thomas Roe and others. The
King tolerated him, and the Calvinist element in England
approved of him for what he represented in their eyes
—the scion of a godly royal house robbed of its heritage
by a Popish tyranny. He had been in England for over
a year when Elizabeth, not without misgiving, decided

to send Rupert after him. No doubt she hoped that his elder brother would influence him by his good example, and she wrote both to him and to various of her friends about the English Court setting out the way in which she hoped he would go.

Rupert arrived in December 1636, and was greeted with masques for which, says a contemporary letter, " high and mighty preparations " had been made. Before long he had easily eclipsed the much duller Charles-Louis. He was gay where Charles-Louis was grave; he was dashing where the other was staid; he was fresh from the battlefield while the other had been hanging about the Court and hob-nobbing with the Puritans for a year; he was carefree while the other was brooding over his lost kingdom and electorate; he was eager to hunt and hawk with the King while the other was for ever hinting and hoping for men and money to regain his throne. The Queen, too—Henrietta Maria—was bored by Charles-Louis and delighted with Rupert. Whether or not Charles-Louis was a prig and a hypocrite, as some say, he was certainly a sneak, for he wrote scandal to his mother about Rupert, whose chief offence was that he had stolen his own thunder, and usurped his place in the affections of the Court.

There is no doubt that Rupert was already the more attractive of the two, apart from his good looks and his great height. There is also no doubt that he was seeing far too much of Henrietta Maria. He was indulging his taste for sport in the company of the King, his taste for drawing and painting in the company of Vandyck and other artists, his taste for a gay life in the company of young bloods about the Court, while Charles-Louis talked theology with dull divines. The Court was bored with Charles-Louis, but it was toying with plans for Rupert. One party wanted to marry him off to the rich daughter of a French duke; another wanted him to lead an expedition to Madagascar, and to be its Governor when captured; Archbishop Laud had the odd idea that he would make an excellent bishop. But Henrietta Maria was out to make him a Catholic, and Rupert himself confessed afterwards that she very nearly succeeded. Elizabeth, with her anxieties fermented by letters to The Hague from Charles-Louis and others, grew frantic, and urged the return of both the brothers; but life in England was pleasant, and Rupert was loath to leave. We read of junketings at Oxford—there is a letter from Wotton to Elizabeth saying that he was looking forward to meeting both Princes there; of hunting at Belvoir in Northamptonshire—Rupert was to benefit long after-wards from his knowledge of its byways and short-cuts; of watching the launching of two pinnaces at the Woolwich dockyard—Phineas Pett, whose family built ships for England for over a century, says that the two brothers watched from the windows of his lodgings " to their great content." But all good things come to an end, and in June 1637 Rupert went out for one last hunt with the King. He said that he wished he could break his neck that morning, so that he could leave his bones in England. The accident he prayed for did not happen, and that evening both brothers sailed for Holland.

Sad as he was to leave England after six such happy

months, Rupert found immediate compensation. The Dutch were besieging Breda, and Maurice was with them. So were many Englishmen; and it was here that Rupert first met various soldiers with whom and against whom he was later to fight in the Civil War—Astley, Wilmot, Goring, Skippon, Monk, Grandison and others. It was the first time that Rupert and Maurice had soldiered together, and they began in characteristic fashion. One foggy evening the two of them crept close up under the walls of the town, and overheard Spaniards of the garrison discussing a forthcoming sortie. The Spanish language had been among their studies at Leyden; the brothers reported what was in the wind; the besiegers were ready for the sally, and it failed disastrously. When the time came for the final assault, Rupert, though forbidden to do so, took a leading part in it, and was one of the first over the walls. Many were killed, Wilmot and Goring were both wounded, but Rupert finished the battle without a scratch.

It was Maurice's turn to be sent back to school by his mother, not this time to Leyden but to Paris. He went the more indignantly because big things were astir. Charles-Louis had long been scraping up resources in order to raise an army of his own. With the death of Gustavus Adolphus much of the fire had gone out of the Thirty Years' War, but the Swedes still had an army at large in Germany. Charles-Louis hoped to achieve something against the Holy Roman Emperor with his own force, and then to join the Swedes. Throughout the summer of 1638 he pressed forward with his preparations, and by September he had a regiment of mounted Guards under Lord Craven, and three of horse, one of them under Rupert. On the frontier of Holland a Swedish contingent under Königsmark joined him; and with the Swedes, as adviser and second-in-command to Charles-Louis, came James King, a Scottish soldier of fortune who had been twenty years in the Swedish service. When the force left Wesel on the Rhine—ten miles from Rheinberg, which Rupert already knew,—it amounted in all to four thouiand men: too many for a raid, too few for a serious campaign.

Rupert always blamed King for the misfortunes of the expedition, and King in fact did not behave very well; but he was an experienced soldier, and in all likelihood he was appalled at the optimism of the Princes and the magnitude of what they hoped to achieve with their tiny army. They marched defiantly eastward into the flat lands of Westphalia, heading for Lemgo, a rich little town, semi-independent, which they believed to be only lightly held. On the way they passed Rheine, which was defended by an Imperial garrison; and Rupert turned aside from the line of march to have a look at it. He found some enemy cavalry outside its gates, and charged them on an impulse—the first cavalry charge of his career. The enemy bolted, and the gates clanged behind them. Charles-Louis witnessed this little action; and perhaps it served to raise still higher the spirits and over-confidence of the two Princes.

They reached Lemgo and prepared to lay siege to it; but within twenty-four hours they were sobered by the news that a much larger Imperial force under General Hatzfeldt was close at hand and marching against them.

Sanguine though they were, this was more than even they were prepared to tackle, and they resolved to make for Minden, where they could shelter under the wing of the main Swedish army. Between Lemgo and Minden lies a long and difficult ridge, covered with forest, and curving like a sickle through that part of Germany; the only pass through it for many miles is the famous Minden Gap, a few hundred yards wide, through which runs the River Weser (and nowadays the railway). One of Julius Cæsar's generals, Quintilius Varus, had fought for it in A.D. 9; British troops were to fight for it in 1759; it has been fought for many times besides. On that October evening of 1638 it was obvious that the Minden Gap offered the only line of retreat to the tiny Palatine army. From Lemgo to the Gap is about fifteen miles, and the route lay through Vlotho. Guns and baggage were sent ahead on the night of the 16th October, and the main body moved on the following morning.

This course of action was not difficult to foresee, and Hatzfeldt must have foreseen it, for he sent a detachment ahead to destroy the bridge over the Weser; and at noon on the 17th, among some hills a little south of Vlotho, he caught the Palatine army. It is said that General King first took up a position on a hill known as the Eiberg, but that Charles-Louis was persuaded by one of his subordinates to draw off into a valley to the north-west. The truth will never be known, though in 1912 a mass grave was discovered on the Eiberg during the making of a new road.

The battle which was now joined lasted three hours, and according to local tradition ranged over a wide area.

The first exchange was when some regiments of Austrian cuirassiers charged the leading Palatinate cavalry, and broke it; then Rupert's regiment charged the Austrians, no doubt while they were disorganised and consolidating, and chased them off the field; and then the Imperialists, making use of their greater numbers and attacking on a wider front, lapped right round the Palatinate troops, cutting off Rupert and such other portions of regiments as were near him. Rupert at one time found himself alone among the enemy, and discovered that they, like he, were wearing white cockades in their helmets, and were mistaking him for one of themselves. Then he saw his brother's standard-bearer beset, and spurred to his rescue. Finding himself once more hemmed in, he put his horse at a hedge, fell, and was taken prisoner. His captor struck up his visor and exclaimed at his youth, asking who he was. " I'm a colonel! " cried Rupert; " A very young one," said the Austrian, who was a colonel himself; but at that moment a soldier came up who knew him by sight, and identified him as Prince Rupert.

The Prince was led away to the rear, and as he went he tentatively opened negotiations with his escort, to see whether he could possibly purchase his release with a bribe. He was making some progress when unfortunately Hatzfeldt himself arrived, to confirm that he had indeed captured one of the Princes and the negotiations came to an abrupt end. At Warendorf Rupert found himself reunited with other prisoners, including Lord Craven, with a bad wound, and Sir Richard Crane, of Craven's Guards. There was no sign of Charles-Louis, James King

or Königsmark. Königsmark and his Swedes had withdrawn—some used a harsher word—at the beginning of
the battle; Charles-Louis and King had fled in a carriage.
They narrowly escaped drowning as they crossed the
flooded Weser, Charles-Louis losing his baggage and the
Garter which Charles of England had given him in
London some years before.[1] He hauled himself out of
the river by a willow-tree, while coachman and horses
were whirled away to their death, and hid in the house
of a local official until he could make his way back to
The Hague. King, who had been wounded, managed to
reach Minden by a roundabout route.

The prisoners were kept for a few days at Warendorf.
Sir Richard Crane was released, by the courtesy of those
times, to carry news of the prisoners to The Hague, where
rumour had it that Rupert had died from many wounds.
Craven was forced to ransom himself for the huge sum of
twenty thousand pounds; he offered more to be allowed
to stay with Rupert, but this was refused. Rupert was
told that he should see the Emperor, to which he retorted
that the Emperor would see him. With an escort of six
hundred musketeers and a like number of cuirassiers
Rupert was carried to Linz, and imprisoned in a grim
castle overlooking the Danube, under Count Von
Kuffstein.

Here he spent nearly three years. Kuffstein was a
kindly jailer, and a friendship sprang up between his
daughter Susan and the tall, romantic young prisoner.
Rupert was able to indulge his taste for tennis, to shoot
and to fence; he pursued his hobbies of drawing and

[1] Just as his father had lost his while fleeing from Prague in 1620.

sketching; he was allowed to pay visits on parole to the castles of neighbouring nobles; and Kuffstein, an old soldier, delighted in helping his studies in the art of war. The British Ambassador at Vienna gave him a poodle as a pet; and this dog, whose name was Boy, was to be his inseparable companion until its death four years later.

The Emperor into whose hands he had fallen was, of course, a fervent Catholic. Perhaps he had heard of Henrietta Maria's attempt to convert Rupert to Catholicism eighteen months before; at all events he caused new efforts to be made now, and the Kuffsteins themselves were converts. The Emperor tried coercion, restricting Rupert's privileges, until induced to forbear by his own brother, who had met and struck up a friendship with Rupert; he also tried persuasion, offering him as an inducement a substantial part of the Lower Palatinate as a petty kingdom. But whatever headway Henrietta Maria had made on him at the Court of England, neither the Stuart nor the Palatine blood in him took kindly to these new methods. Even when he was offered his release in exchange for merely asking the Emperor's pardon for taking up arms against the Imperial Crown, Rupert refused.

Elizabeth had been thoroughly pessimistic about his fate from the start. At first she would not believe that he was alive; then she was quite sure that he would be persuaded to join the Church of Rome. Constantly she urged her brother of England to do something; and at last Sir Thomas Roe was sent on a special embassy to Vienna to negotiate his release. Roe was tactful in his dealings both with the Emperor and the prickly Prince.

The former consented to be satisfied with an undertaking that Rupert would never again take up arms against the Holy Roman Empire, and the latter pledged his word. He returned to Holland by way of Prague, which he had never seen since he was borne away from it, as a howling baby, twenty-one years before; and he burst into his mother's house a few days before Christmas 1641, and a few minutes before the arrival of a courier bringing word of his release.

* 2 *

Edgehill and After

RUPERT HAD been home for less than three weeks when serious news came from England. On the 4th of January, 1642, King Charles had gone down to the House of Commons to arrest the Five Members whom he was endeavouring to impeach. He had left his retinue in Westminster Hall, and entered the House of Commons—accompanied by, of all people, Charles-Louis—to find, in his own phrase, that his " birds had flown." War was perceptibly nearer; London, the Home Counties, the Navy were all aroused against the King; and on the 10th Charles had found it wise to leave Whitehall for Hampton Court.

Early in February Rupert crossed to Dover, giving as his excuse that he wanted to thank his uncle for obtaining his release from the Emperor's prison. It is much more likely that his true reason was to put his sword at Charles's disposal. At Dover he found the King, Henrietta Maria and their daughter Mary, who was on her way to marry the Prince of Orange. The Queen was to accompany her, and in the Queen's baggage were the Crown Jewels. For a long time the King was closeted with Rupert. He explained that he still hoped to preserve peace. If

Rupert with his military reputation were to join him now, Parliament might think he had decided on war, and intensify its preparations, whereas there was still hope of peace. Rupert could best serve him at this stage by escorting the Queen to Holland, and awaiting developments.

So to Holland he returned; and while the Queen raised money on the Continent by selling some of the Crown Jewels, while the King gathered his supporters about him at York (whither he had gone from Hampton Court), while Parliament stifled loyal opposition in the Home Counties, Rupert chafed at The Hague. But in August, Henrietta Maria sent for him, handed him his commission as General of the Horse, and bade him make for England with all speed.

It was not in the character of Rupert to appreciate the tragedy of the situation now bubbling up in England. He was not yet twenty-three; he loved fighting for the sake of adventure, and he adored his uncle. He was quite untroubled by any regret that Englishmen would soon be fighting Englishmen. To him the King was the King, and to oppose him was high treason. He could not appreciate the cruel conflict of loyalties which was distressing so many. Sir William Waller and Sir Ralph Hopton—the same Hopton who had carried Rupert's mother away from Prague—had been friends for many years; Hopton declared for the King, Waller for Parliament; but Waller wrote to Hopton that his affection was unchangeable and his friendship inviolable, saying: " Let us play our parts in this tragedy in a way of honour and without personal animosities." Sir Edmund Verney disapproved of the King's actions, but, although one of his sons followed the Parliament, Sir Edmund himself said: " I have eaten the King's bread and served him near thirty years; I will not do so base a thing as to forsake him." And Lord Paget, who had hitherto supported the Parliament against the King, now joined him at York, and issued the following brief statement on a single printed sheet:

It may seeme strange that I, who with all zeale and earnestnesse have prosecuted in the beginning of this Parliament, the Reformation of all disorders in Church, and Commonwealth, should now in a time of such great distractions, desert the cause. Most true it is, that my ends were the common good: and whilst that was prosecuted, I was ready to lay down both my life and fortune: But when I found a Preparation of Armes against the KING, under the shadow of Loyaltie, I rather resolved to obey a good Conscience than particular ends, and am now on my way to His Majesty, where I will throw myself downe at his feet, and die a loyal Subject.

PAGET[1]

In Rupert's eyes Englishmen at this hour had the choice of being Royalists or traitors; there were no gradations of loyalty for him. On his first visit to England, six years before, his mother had written to a friend at Whitehall: " He is still a little giddy, though

[1] A copy of this broadsheet is preserved in the College Library at Eton, where my attention was drawn to it by Mr. Robert Birley. I have not seen it mentioned elsewhere.

not so much as he has been. Pray tell him when he does ill, for he is good-natured enough, but does not always think." There was no restraining him now, for he smelled the battle like a horse among the trumpets. He collected Maurice, and essayed to sail in the *Lion*, the same English ship as had brought him over with Henrietta Maria; but the weather and the ship's captain were alike against him, and the crossing was finally made in a vessel lent by the Prince of Orange.

Parliament held most of the ports of England; but in the north, where Lord Newcastle was stoutly for the King, the port of Tynemouth was safe in Royalist hands. A Parliamentary squadron of three ships gave chase off Flamborough Head, but desisted when in sight of Tynemouth. All his life Rupert was a poor sailor; he had been ill on his previous short crossings of the Channel, but on this longer voyage he suffered abominably. Once ashore his spirits and health returned to him, and learning that the King was at Nottingham he set off immediately to join him, with Maurice and others. By a freak of August weather there was a frost, but he determined all the same to ride through the night, and was not even deterred from his purpose when his horse fell and he put his shoulder out. Within three hours he had had it set, and was again in the saddle heading south.

At Nottingham they learned that the King had marched against Coventry. They snatched a few hours' sleep and then rode on. Soon they heard that he was in Leicester, and turning aside off the Coventry road they found him. Charles had had a rebuff at Coventry and his cavalry under Wilmot had done rather ingloriously in a minor skirmish. The Royal uncle and the loyal nephew dined and slept at Lady Devon's, and Rupert took immediate command of the eight hundred ill-equipped cavalry in the royal column. Next morning they rode back to Nottingham together; and there the Standard of England was raised.

It was a sadly inauspicious ceremony. The weather was wild, and it took twenty men to support the Standard, while two thousand troops shivered in the rain. The King, still in vague hopes of staving off the ultimate disaster of actual war, chose to alter the terms of his Proclamation at the last moment, and kept the Herald waiting while he made erasures and alterations so involved that the Herald had difficulty in deciphering them as he read. At last the Standard was hoisted over the Castle, showing the arms of England on one side and a portrait of Charles on the other: but the weather worsened during the night, and next morning the Standard of England was found to have fallen. It was re-erected in a park.

Of all those about the King at this time, there is no doubt that Rupert had the highest reputation as a soldier. Admire him as we may—and we cannot help it—it is worth considering how far it was deserved. Ten years earlier, as a boy of thirteen, he had witnessed the short campaign against Rheinberg. Since then he had witnessed four sieges, had fought a skirmish lasting a matter of minutes outside Rheine, and shared in the disaster of a short autumn afternoon at Vlotho. He had shown personal enterprise and gallantry and a good tactical sense. He had never had to make a strategical decision; and he cared nothing for political considerations, a burden which commanders of all ages have had to carry in varying degrees, as a racehorse carries weight. Considering how little experience he really had, it is astonishing how great his reputation was and it is the more to his credit that he enhanced it so quickly by fresh and indisputable successes. His reputation and his successes together ensured within a few months that the mere hint of his possible appearance in a certain area was enough to cause elaborate marching and counter-marching among the Parliamentary forces.

Temperamentally he was more of a commando leader, in the modern sense, than a true higher commander. When he was near the King, he had more influence with him than any other of Charles's advisers, whether military or civil; yet in the early stages of the war, when that influence was at its greatest, he used it almost exclusively in favour of his own command. To use another modern phrase, his command became a " private army " within the whole; and " private armies " are always distinguished by two characteristics: loyalty to their commander from within, and jealousy from without. Whenever he had to leave Charles's side, the whispers of his enemies began, and the decisions which he had won were overturned. Rupert was a born commander and a bad subordinate; Charles was a born vacillator, to whom the latest advice seemed always the soundest.

The Royalist direction of the Civil War makes a sad story of petty jealousies, confused counsels, irresolution, intrigue and even treachery. If Rupert had been ten years more mature, all might have been well. There were plenty of sound men among the King's advisers, and if Rupert had been wise enough to seek them out and win their trust he might have moulded them into a solid, sensible and dependable council. Charm he had in plenty, but wisdom he lacked. He alienated Hyde the Chancellor, Lindsey the Commander-in-Chief, and others of the old guard by his impatience and lack of tact; he accepted as allies for a moment those who supported his plans of the moment, and made no attempt to come to terms with those who, knowing that he was a great favourite of the King, were bound to be jealous at first. All his energies went into the training and handling of his cavalry, into finding them battles to win, and into getting them the best of what little was going. As for his brother Maurice, he was a boor with only two attractive qualities: his undoubted gallantry and his unquestioning devotion to his brother. And Rupert's devotion to him—for he could do no wrong in Rupert's eyes—was another cause of friction among those whom it was Rupert's duty to placate.

Rupert's first open quarrel was with Lord Digby. A trivial incident while Rupert was passing through Nottingham on his original journey towards the King had given him a poor opinion of this not very honourable peer. Soon Digby made some slighting reference to Rupert's taste for low company. The truth seems to be that both Rupert and Maurice preferred to spend their time in the training and company of their rather miscellaneous cavalry than in dicing and wining with Digby, Wilmot, Goring and the other more raffish members of the King's circle. The squabble was patched up by a written apology, and Digby actually took service under Rupert for a few weeks until he was wounded; but he never lost a chance to undermine Rupert's position with the King, and was ultimately Rupert's downfall. Nor was Goring, still lame from his wound at Breda, and now in the process of surrendering Portsmouth to the King's enemies, beloved of Rupert; nor Wilmot, who had commanded the cavalry until Rupert's coming, and was still serving as his subordinate.

Hyde and Lindsey soon had grounds for their fears that Rupert was irresponsible. Only a fortnight after his arrival he rode into Leicester, one of the richest towns in England, which had as yet decided neither for the King nor for Parliament, but whose adherence to either cause was a matter of moment. He caused a letter to be delivered to the Mayor calling on him for an immediate loan from the city of two thousand pounds for the King, " for the safeguard of his Royall person agaynst the rebellious insurrections of the true malignant party." To encourage the Mayor, he added a postscript to say that: " If any disaffected persons with you shall refuse themselves, or perswade you, to neglect this command, I shall tomorrow appeare before your towne in such a posture with horse, foot and cannon, as shall make you knowe 'tis more safe to obey than resist his Majestie's commands."

Hyde was horrified, and so was the King; and a hasty letter from Charles sought to placate the Mayor and Aldermen. He had seen Rupert's letter, which " Wee doe utterly disavowe and dislike, being written without our privity and consent. Soe Wee doe hereby absolutely free and discharge you and that our Towne from yielding any obedience to the same, and by our own Letters to our said nephew Wee have written to him presently to revoke the same, as being an Act very displeasing to Us. . . . Wee should have taken it well from any of Our subjects that would voluntarily assist Us with ye loan of armes or money. But it is so farre from Our hart or intention by menaces to compell any to it, as Wee abhorre ye thought of it."

Rupert's letter is dated the 6th, Charles's the 8th, of September; but there also exists, dated the 9th, Rupert's receipt to the Mayor, bailiffs and burgesses of Leicester, for the sum of £500 loaned to His Majesty; so it seems that his ride was not for nothing, and that he obtained his results before the King had time to mitigate the force of his demands. Rupert only recognised one kind of war, whether in England or on the Continent, whether with mercenaries or with men fighting for a cause. Controversy for him was always etched in black and white ; there were no shades of grey. At the same time his sense of chivalry and of what might be called the etiquette of arms was as highly developed as any in his day. His very first brush, an attack on the house of an absent Parliamentarian, ended when he discovered that it was being defended by its mistress: he congratulated her on her spirited performance, and withdrew.

Two weeks later he was nearly caught napping. With a small body of horse, he was resting in a field near Powicke Bridge, on the outskirts of Worcester, when a much bigger body of Parliamentary cavalry stumbled on them. There was no time to set his troop in order.

With such officers and men as were handy, he leapt on to his horse and charged. The Roundheads broke and galloped away, leaving their two senior officers as prisoners. Wilmot was wounded in the side, Maurice badly in the head, but the rout was complete, and Rupert sent the Parliamentary colours to the King as the fruits of his first operation in his uncle's service. It was from this moment that stories began to circulate of his wanderings in disguise in and out of Roundhead camps; he was even reported to have sold apples to Roundhead soldiers, disguised as a yokel. Parliamentary presses issued diatribes ascribing atrocities to " Prince Robber," and the more credulous insisted that he was a warlock, with Boy the poodle for his familiar spirit. The Royalists hailed his successes with joy; as early as the 5th of September a letter from Oxford reported that " the scholars generally feed themselves with an expectation of Prince Rupert's coming to their aid with a great army."

At first sight, the Civil War seems to have no apparent strategy, but on closer examination a pattern takes shape. To generalise is dangerous, but very roughly the North and West were for the King, the East and South for the Parliament: those towns which were centres of commerce were for the Parliament, and cathedral cities, with their ecclesiastical allegiance, for the King. In the counties held by Parliament dissension was rigorously suppressed, in those held for the King it could never be wholly stamped out. Many individuals abstained from supporting either side, and later in the war there arose the phenomenon of the Clubmen, country folk who were goaded by the depredations of both armies into resisting all comers. The two sides were not so clear-cut as the definitions of " Royalist " and " Parliamentarian " would have one believe: 25 per cent of the peers came out for the Parliament, and 35 per cent of the Commons for the King.

London itself, though chiefly for the Parliament, contained Royalist sympathisers, and others who were prepared to hail the winner with enthusiasm, to whichever side he might belong. And London was at once the main base of the Parliament and the true objective of the Royalists. It was the greatest port of the Kingdom as well as the seat of Government. From London the main roads radiated, and into London came barges as well as ships, down the Thames as well as up its estuary. Much of the fighting can therefore be related to London: the raids and battles in and near the Thames Valley directly so. Then there were the fights for other communications, for the towns commanding the routes into Wales, where the King had an important source of manpower, and for the routes linking his forces in the north with those in the west. On the King's side, throughout the war, apart from a general intention to capture London, there was lacking the supreme essential of any campaign: an overriding plan or policy to which all else was to be subordinated.[1] The object of Parliament, on the other hand, was clearly defined: to bring the King's Army to battle and to destroy it. There were many on the side of Parliament who still looked upon

[1] The principle of war known in military circles as " The Maintenance of the Objective."

the King as their sovereign, and their task as a mission
to separate him from his evil counsellors. When the war
had already been some months in progress, the Royalist
battle-cry was: " For God and the King ! " and that of
the Roundheads: " For King and Parliament! "

For munitions, Parliament was better off than Charles.
They had the main arsenals of London and Cambridge,
while the King had the minor one of Nottingham and
the fruits of Henrietta Maria's jewels. The Navy was
for the Parliament almost to a ship.

At the outset of the war, before the bickerings of the
Court divided counsel, and before the various feuds and
quarrels in which Rupert was beginning to engage had
begun to undermine his position with the King, Rupert
got his own way; and even if he were no strategist his
first instinct was militarily sound: to make for London
as the seat of government and the centre of disaffection.
Charles at first fell in with this policy, and during the
first weeks of October he concentrated his forces at
Shrewsbury. Lord Essex, with the Parliamentary army,
was at Worcester, when he suddenly became aware that
the King, advised by Rupert, was on the move. The
news reached London also, and barricades and earth-
works were thrown up with feverish haste.

Essex's task—to interpose his army between the King's
and London—was clear enough, but it might be thought
that the wide choice of routes before the King would
make it difficult for Essex to know which he would take.
On Rupert's advice the King had chosen to move by
way of Birmingham, Kenilworth and Banbury; Essex,
with what appeared to be a good guess, marched due

east, through Stratford-on-Avon to Kineton. On the night of the 22nd of October, the King's evening council had just broken up when news came that an outpost of Rupert's horsemen, seeking billets at Wormleighton a few miles ahead, had surprised and captured a party of Essex's men engaged on the same errand. The prisoners disclosed the location of Essex's force, and at Rupert's suggestion the King gave orders for the army to be drawn up on the long ridge of Edgehill, confirming that he had done so in a note dated 4 a.m. on the 23rd of October.

By 8 a.m. the two armies faced each other, that of Essex looking up the slope towards the King's array. Neither was yet complete: Essex was waiting for more infantry under Hampden, and the King for his artillery. During the long morning an argument developed among the Royalist commanders about the tactics to be employed. Rupert wanted to be allowed to try and break the enemy by shock tactics, as practised by Gustavus Adolphus. Lord Lindsey, the Commander-in-Chief, preferred the more stolid methods of attack favoured by the Dutch, in which the cavalry used to halt and discharge its firearms before coming to grips with the enemy. Apart from his natural preference for the spectacular, there were two arguments in favour of Rupert's advice: he knew his cavalry's limitations in training, and may well have considered that they were more likely to succeed in a passionate charge than in a slow, opposed advance; and he was painfully aware of their deficiencies in firearms. It is an accepted axiom to-day that speed is one of the best forms of protection for a mobile army; but in the seventeenth century Gustavus Adolphus was the first to restore mobility to the cavalry by lightening the load on the horse's back at the expense of the armour on the horseman's person; and his methods, though regarded with respect, still savoured of military heresy.

Rupert gained the King's consent; and Lord Lindsey resigned his command, preferring to take command of his own Lincolnshire regiment than to fight the whole battle on a plan of which he disapproved. Lord Lindsey's son, who was one of Rupert's officers, chose to follow his father. The vacant command was accepted by Lord Ruthven, who having himself fought under Gustavus Adolphus agreed with Rupert's views. So Rupert, no doubt with memories of Rheine and the opening stages of the fight at Vlotho, rode along the whole length of his line telling his men what to do: they were to go for the enemy at full gallop, sword in hand, keeping in line, and paying no heed to the enemy's fire.

At three o'clock in the afternoon Essex's guns opened fire, and those of the King replied. Then Rupert's own wing of the cavalry on the left and Wilmot's on the right charged down the hill and along the low ground towards Kineton, with the main road between them. The Parliamentary cavalry broke and ran; some of them, including a colonel, are said to have ridden fifty miles that evening in their terror. But not all: there was a disciplined body of Scottish cavalry under Sir William Balfour of Pitcullo which instead of being on the flanks was held in reserve behind the main body of infantry. As the Royalist cavalry pursued to Kineton, the Roundhead infantry closed for the main battle, and Balfour's cavalry passed round the Royalists and harried their rear. For a time things were critical and some faint hearts tried to persuade the King to leave the field. The fighting was most desperate around the Standard. Sir Edmund Verney the Standard Bearer, the head of one of the most honoured families of England, was killed as he defended it; he continued to clutch its pole even in death, until a Roundhead severed his hand at the wrist and carried off the Standard, hand and all. It was recovered later in the day by a ruse; and the ring which was on his hand that day is still preserved by his family in his old home.

At last the cavalry came back, blown but triumphant, and the Roundhead infantry disengaged. Hampden's reinforcements had by now arrived, but the rest of the infantry were in confusion, and had to be covered by Balfour's cavalry as they withdrew. Somebody suggested to Wilmot, whose horses were less exhausted than Rupert's, that he should charge and break Balfour's men, to allow the Royalist infantry to get in and complete the rout; but he replied that he would prefer to live and enjoy the fruits of the day.

So the two armies drew apart, and settled down to endure the bitterly cold night. Each side believed that the other had had the best of the day, no uncommon thing in war; and each feared that the other might renew battle with a surprise in the night. They built watch-fires and huddled round them and thought about their dead. The losses on both sides had been heavy. Sir Ralph Verney, the Roundhead son of the Standard Bearer, trying in vain some weeks after the battle to find out what had become of his father's body, learned that over four thousand corpses had been buried. Edmund Ludlow, who fought in a Roundhead regiment, wrote that sixty Royalists lay " within the compass of three-score yards about the Standard; " he noted also that

the greatest slaughter on his side had been among those
that ran away, whereas the greatest on the King's side
had been among those who stood their ground. Among
the Royalist dead was Lord Lindsey.

The doubt as to who had won the battle was reflected
in the messages reaching London. One report included
Rupert among the dead. On the day after the battle
the rival armies continued to face each other, but neither
made a move to resume it. On the second day, however,
Rupert's patrols established that Essex was drawing off.
He caught up with the rearguards in Kineton, capturing
baggage and the whole of Essex's correspondence. Among
it was the explanation of how Essex had been able to
make such an accurate forecast of the movements of the
Royal army: his letters included full reports from
Rupert's own secretary, one Blake, together with a
request for an increase in his pay as a spy. Blake was
hanged a few days later at Oxford.

In truth, of course, it was the King who had won the
day; for Rupert was able to report that Essex was
moving northwards: the road to London was therefore
open. Rupert at once suggested that he should press on
with his three thousand cavalry, seize Westminster and
Whitehall, and hold them until the main body could
arrive. He pointed out that the will of the Parliament
to resist would be at its lowest ebb when the news of
Edgehill reached London, and we know now that the
mood of London was exactly as he pictured it. But
despite the brilliant vindication of his judgment on the
morning of Edgehill, his rivals among the King's advisers
were too strong for him. Lord Bristol, Digby's father,

persuaded Charles that Rupert was not to be trusted in London: he would pillage it for a certainty. No doubt the Leicester episode was quoted once more as an additional argument for this forecast.

In this moment of indecision Charles lost the war. Even if he had moved on to London at his own pace, with Rupert in leash beside him, he could have covered the eighty miles in four days at the most. As it was, he withstood Rupert's eager pleadings. Next day he took a right fork instead of a left, and plodded ponderously through Banbury to Oxford, which he reached by slow stages on the 29th. And while he dallied in Oxford Essex passed him by, and set to work to prepare London for defence.

The loyal expectations of the scholars of Oxford were now realised. The King set up his quarters in Christ Church, where Rupert stayed with him at first; later the Prince moved to Magdalen. As the King settled down and his Court gathered round him, Rupert made a series of sweeps about the countryside, partly for forage and partly to maintain a screen of activity. Operating at first from Abingdon, he occupied Aylesbury, in front of which he got involved in a skirmish, of which he had rather the worst, with Balfour of Pitcullo. Undaunted he withdrew to Maidenhead, and from there tried to storm Windsor Castle, which, if he had succeeded, would have given him control of the Thames and prevented barge traffic reaching London from the west. Windsor proving too much for him, he rode by Staines to Kingston, where he thought he might build a fort to serve the same purpose; but the trained bands (militia)

Cropredy

Banbury

Newport Pagnell

Buckingham

R. Cherwell

Bletchingdon
Brill

Aylesbury

Oxford
Tetsworth
Chislehampton
Thame
Chinnor
Lewknor
Chalgrove

Abingdon

Wallingford

Henley

R. Thames

Maidenhead

Brentford
Turnham Green
Colnbrook

Windsor
Hounslow
Egham
Staines
Putney

Reading

Newbury

R. Kennet
Aldermarston

Basing

Basingstoke

Scale of Miles

0   5   10   20

of two counties were ready and waiting for him, in close
country and behind hedges where he could not get at
them. Still based on Maidenhead, he rode out towards
Colnbrook, which he found almost undefended; he made
a firm base of it, realising its value in any attack on
London. All these operations had taken little over a
week; they had dazzled his opponents by their speed;

and they had produced invaluable information about routes and garrisons.

The King was now moving in a gingerly fashion down the Thames Valley, still wasting time in fruitless negotiations with the Parliament. Reading fell, and Henley; and on the 11th of November the King reached Colnbrook. That evening Rupert was at Egham, where a couple of Roundhead merchants had been detained and brought before him for interrogation. They have left us a vivid little picture. The Prince was in bed with all his clothes on. One of the men had a hat with " favours " stuck in it, which the Prince examined. He remarked that he saw no sign of the King's colours, but smiled when the owner confessed that they were those of his sweetheart. They saw him again next morning on Hounslow Heath; they were still in custody when they caught sight of him talking to none other than the King. He was apparently arguing, for he kept scratching his head and tearing his hair, " as if in some grave discontent." As he talked, he took off his scarlet jacket, which he handed to his servant, and put on a grey one instead. No doubt he was getting ready for action, for he was about to assault Brentford.

The cavalry attack on Brentford failed, for the enemy had ensconced themselves behind barricades of rubble, wagons and furniture, which were still more effective than the hedges of Kingston. Thrusting his horse to the rear, Rupert took command of the leading infantry—a regiment of Welshmen which had not shone at Edgehill —and led his first charge on foot since the assault at Breda five years before. The barricades were torn down, the furious Welshmen poured through, and the entire garrison was chased either into the river or along the road to London, leaving fifteen guns and several hundred prisoners.

But next day, at Turnham Green, saw the fading of Charles's last hopes of victory, had he only known it, and the payment of the price of his failure to march on London after Edgehill. He could and should have arrived on the 29th of October; now it was the 13th of November, and the fortnight's grace had been put to good account; now the trained bands of London, twenty-four thousand strong, were drawn up on Turnham Green, sullenly facing the King. They were determined, disciplined, well-appointed and well-commanded: Skippon was their Major-General, and he addressed them all in simple and confident words: " Come, my honest, brave boys, pray heartily, and fight heartily, and God will bless us." The Royal troops were ordered to withdraw with Sir Jacob Astley in command as far as the river. There Rupert sat his horse, standing in the water, encouraging his men, and holding the bridgehead until the last man was over it. The Roundheads made no attempt to harass their retreat beyond the bridge, although downstream at Putney they had built another bridge of boats, over which they might well have passed an army for that purpose. The Royalists withdrew slowly by way of Reading to Oxford.

The King now thought it time to go into winter quarters, and settled down comfortably at Christ Church. He left to Rupert the task of deciding which of the towns about Oxford should be garrisoned. Troops were put into Abingdon, Wallingford, Brill, Bletchingdon and Banbury; and there were outposts at Reading, Basing and elsewhere. Hyde had the far more difficult problem of dealing with the Royal finances; he was paying out three thousand pounds a week. A mint was set up in Oxford, into which was poured all the silver plate which was being pressed upon the King by loyalists and surrendered to him by unwilling supporters. Only those in Oxford received regular pay from Hyde's coffers; those who rode out on raids depended on loot; those who were quartered in garrisons were restricted to what they could find in their own immediate neighbourhood. Financially, therefore, those soldiers who were most actively engaged in fighting fared the best. In modern warfare it is usually the other way round.

* 3 *

Marston Moor

IT IS unlikely that Rupert found the gaieties of Oxford at Christmas—which were considerable—much to his taste. For one thing, plans for the coming year were fermenting in his mind; and for another the commanders of his outposts were for ever pestering him with impossible demands—for boots, clothing, munitions, and sometimes to be relieved from irksome duties. There was little discipline among them and they thought nothing of riding in to Oxford to see their friends. His relations with some of them were severely strained. When he ordered Wilmot to occupy Marlborough, he received a reply which must have infuriated him with its languid impertinence, though the order was obeyed. Nor was he getting on any better with the dandies about the Court. He did, however, make two or three staunch friends: Nicholas, the King's Secretary; his own cousin, the Duke of Richmond; and above all William Legge. " Honest Will " was a man of an integrity remarkable in that age, unswervingly faithful, beloved by everyone and without an enemy in the world. His father had sailed with Walter Raleigh; he himself had seen much service with the Dutch; he was to spend most of his life in prison for his loyalty; and eventually he refused a peerage, which was later conferred for his own services upon his son. He had been taken prisoner early in the war, but had escaped. Rupert and he had already met at Nottingham, but it was at Oxford that the friendship began which was never to be clouded.

The attempt against London having failed, a new strategic plan was devised for 1643. Newcastle's army from the north and Sir Ralph Hopton's from Devon and Cornwall were to converge on London, the former by way of East Anglia towards the Essex side of the Thames estuary, the latter through Kent (where some support was looked for) to its southern side. London would thus be cut off from the Continent, and completely surrounded. Apart from the other difficulties of this plan, nobody appreciated the reluctance of the Northerners and West-countrymen to move so far from their own lands, and to leave their homes unprotected.

It was desirable also to secure the lines of communication between the North and the West, and those into the recruiting area of Wales. These were impeded at the moment by the Parliamentary occupation of Bristol, Cirencester, Birmingham and other towns lying at important road-junctions, while nearer home the Roundheads were in enough strength to make a serious though unsuccessful assault on the Royalist outpost at Brill, only ten miles from Oxford.

Rupert's first move was against Cirencester. He had spent from Christmas Eve to Twelfth Night at Oxford, when he rode out with Lord Hertford, who had been urging on the King the desirability of reducing Cirencester. Maurice was with him. Between them they had six thousand horse and foot, and they boldly summoned the defenders to surrender, which the defenders refused to do. The Royalists drew off for the moment, but a fortnight later returned, and enticed some of the garrison out of the town by an ingenious feint on a neighbouring castle. Their assault then succeeded, and Rupert had gained not only an important town, but large supplies of cloth in which to attire the King's army.

Rupert next reconnoitred other towns, including Gloucester and Warwick; and after a few days' office-work, as we should call it, in Oxford, set out again on his tireless tour of garrisons. On the 4th of March he left Cirencester by easy stages for Bristol, where two merchants, Bourcher and Yeoman, had undertaken to open the gates to him; but the plot miscarried; Bourcher and Yeoman, the two merchants, were executed: Rupert returned to Oxford for a single night; emerged again for three days and " a little Skirmish before Aylesbury "; and once more back to Oxford.

On the 22nd of March, Queen Henrietta Maria landed at Bridlington, with stores and munitions for the King. She too had been chased by Parliament ships, under a Captain Batten, who having just missed her at sea bombarded the town as she lay asleep in it—an incident which was to cause him embarrassment when he changed his allegiance later on. The problem now was how to bring her south, along with her precious stores. She would need a strong escort if she were to thread her way safely between hostile garrisons along the roads; and there was the additional danger of a pounce by

Essex from the east. At the same time, Lord Derby and others were hard pressed in Lancashire and Cheshire. If Rupert were to march north, he could not only relieve the pressure on Lord Derby but also bring back the Queen; and accordingly he set out at the beginning of April with six hundred foot and twice as many horse.

By now any move by Rupert was guaranteed to spread nervousness among the Parliamentarians. Only a few days before, at the news of the skirmish at Aylesbury sixty miles away, " the alarm was so hotly given at Cambridge that the Five Associated Counties sent some thousands of men into the town " and sent for Cromwell post-haste from Norfolk to come and defend it, which he did. This time it was Birmingham's turn. When the inhabitants and garrison of Birmingham heard that Rupert was first at Stratford, and next at Henley-in-Arden, they knew he was heading their way, and their guilty consciences feared the worst: for they had plundered royal plate and imprisoned royal servants after the King's journey through their town seven months before. The Cavaliers' assault was opposed, but quickly successful, though it cost the life of Lord Denbigh, one of the most honourable of the King's supporters. His son, like Sir Edmund Verney's, was on the Roundhead side, but, more fortunate, he managed to find and bury his father's body.

Lichfield, which had been captured by the Parliament only a month earlier, was Rupert's next objective. Here the garrison was more numerous and the town more defensible than at Birmingham. The Cathedral itself, sadly profaned, had been made into a fortress, and there was a moat about the town walls. But Rupert was too resourceful a soldier to be checked by this; he drained the moat, enlisted miners from the coalpits in the neighbouring town of Tamworth, called for volunteers to help them, and after ten days sprang the first mine ever sprung in England. The first assault on the breach failed with heavy loss, but the Prince then caused his guns to fire through it, and the besiegers surrendered. By holding out for the better part of a fortnight they had greatly delayed Rupert's march; and during the last few days he had been overtaken by a series of letters from Charles showing increasing anxiety about the defence of Reading. At last came a definite order to return and raise the siege, and he hurried south, leaving a garrison in Lichfield.

Unfortunately he arrived too late. Aston, the Governor of Reading, was normally stout-hearted, and he had three thousand men in the town; but he had complained in a letter to Rupert that they were poor stuff, and that he wished he had some German soldiers in their place. Around the town were twenty thousand Roundhead troops, and little hope of relief; and when Aston was knocked out by a tile falling on his head, the command passed to Colonel Fielding, who decided to surrender. In the middle of his parley and to his great dismay, Rupert's relieving force, which neither he nor Aston had expected, arrived to give battle to the besiegers. Fielding was urged by his officers to take part in the fight, but in the circumstances he thought it incompatible with his honour. Rupert withdrew, and Fielding and his garrison marched out with the honours of war. He was condemned to death by court martial, but reprieved on the plea of the Prince of Wales—instigated, so it is said, by Rupert.

The times were too uncertain for Rupert to resume his interrupted march to the North, and he reverted to his old role of screening Oxford. The bickerings of the Court and the intrigues of its hangers-on were no better, and were soon to get worse. Rupert's distrust of what was going on behind his back was no mere freak of " persecution mania." On the 11th of May, in a long letter dealing largely with his own troubles, and bewailing among other things the unchecked prevalence of duelling among officers at Oxford, Secretary Nicholas wrote:

I could wish that some busybodies would not meddle, as they do, with other people's offices; and that the King would leave every officer respectively to look after his own charge; and that His Majesty would content himself to overlook all men, and see that each did his duty in his proper place; which would give abundant satisfaction, and quiet those that are jealous to see some men meddle who have nothing to do with affairs.

On the 17th of June Rupert rode out of Oxford on an expedition which was after his own heart and which remains a classic of its kind. The commander of his outpost at Abingdon had sent him intelligence that Essex was on the move in a direction which would take him north-east of Oxford, and this news was confirmed by Hurry, a Roundhead colonel, who chose this moment

to change sides, adding that a convoy with the soldiers'
pay was on its way to join Essex. Leaving Oxford in the
late afternoon with a thousand horse, and preceded by
an advanced guard under Will Legge, he arrived before
dawn, after some hours' rest for the horses, in a group
of villages close under the Chiltern Hills. He burst
through the enemy's outpost at Tetsworth without
deigning to reply to the fire of the troops billeted in it;
in Lewknor, which he reached at first light, he took
prisoners; in Chinnor, he took more prisoners, and made
a killing. But he could not locate the treasure, and the
Roundheads had been effectively roused. He was in
their rear area, where the look-out kept was slack and
unwatchful; but the main body was turning back to
deal with him, and he made haste to the south-west.
Between seven and eight in the morning, having beaten
off the immediate pursuit, he rested for an hour in a
field near Chalgrove, sending some dragoons ahead to
hold the crossing over the river at Chiselhampton,
and to lay an ambush short of it. Enemy cavalry was
now advancing on him; they were in no hurry, for they
wished to give time to their main body to interpose
between Rupert and his route of escape at Chiselhampton;
and Rupert watched them manœuvring into position
with undisturbed calm. Then, as they opened fire, he
said: " This insolency is not to be borne! " and putting
spurs to his horse was first over the hedge and among
them. Other squadrons took the enemy on either flank,
and most of the Roundheads fled.

At this moment the noble Parliamentarian Hampden
arrived from the grounds of Warpsgrove House, a few

hundred yards to the north, and tried to stem the rot; but he was immediately hit with two bullets, and rode painfully off the field to die. Among the many ironies of the Civil War, none is more bitter than this: that, twenty-five years before, Hampden had written a congratulatory Ode on the marriage of Rupert's mother, wishing her an illustrious progeny as its fruit. It was at the hand of that progeny that he died. Meanwhile, Rupert led his force without interruption across the river at Chiselhampton, and jogged homeward to Oxford, without the treasure that he had gone out to seek, but having, in the course of a short summer night and morning, wrought havoc and disorder for the loss of twelve men. He brought with him prisoners and colours, and many of his troopers were leading captured horses. This exploit and that of Jeb Stuart in the Civil War in America stand in a class by themselves as cavalry raids.

The time was now judged opportune for the Queen to move south. For some time she had been at Newark, whose strong castle on the River Trent is a familiar sight to those who travel to Scotland by train. She had no need of Rupert to convoy her, for she had for her own protection, and that of the hundred and thirty wagon-loads of stores which she was bringing, three thousand foot and thirty " companies " of horse. As " Commander-in-Chief " she had the profligate Harry Jermyn —whose son was afterwards notorious for being drunk for five years—but she described herself as " she-Majesty generalissima over all, and extremely diligent am I." She proposed to move with caution well to the west, and she asked the King to " have a care that no troop

of Essex's army incommodate us." Rupert set himself
the task of flank guard, and moved out on the 1st of
July to Thornton Park, near Buckingham, from which
roads radiated in every direction in which he might
need to move. The owner, a Parliamentarian country
gentleman, was described afterwards as "much taken
with his courtesy," and Rupert made the most of his
time there. He went out shooting on foot, killing five
buck, which his dog Boy pulled down. Two "alarms"
are reported, which may have been identical: in the one
case he is said to have shifted his quarters out of doors
for the night, in the other to have heard of the enemy's
approach while he was shaving, to have routed them,
and then returned to his razor. He succeeded, at least,
in perpetually harassing the enemy until, in his own
words, they were wearied of their lives.

One day the Roundheads found that their tormentor
had disappeared. He had in fact gone north-west to
Stratford-on-Avon, where he met the Queen. On the
13th of July they were joined by the King, near the field
of Edgehill, and the whole party, wagons and all,
moved back together without interference to Oxford,
where the King and Queen set up their quarters in
Merton College.

There was other news to add to the happiness of this
reunion. Hopton and Maurice had won a battle at
Lansdowne in Dorset; and while Hopton recovered from
a wound, Maurice followed it up with another victory at
Roundway Down, just north of Devizes. The moment
had come for another attempt on Bristol, and on the
20th of July Rupert and Maurice merged their forces

for a joint and determined assault. (7th July at Buckingham; 11th at Stratford; 13th at Edgehill; and 20th
at Stroud, with a visit to Oxford in between: it is worth
noting Rupert's energy when there was work to be
done, in contrast with the dilatory habits of some of his
fellow commanders.) On Sunday the 23rd he settled
down his force at Westbury, two miles north of Bristol,
and rode in the afternoon with Maurice and others up
the River Avon to Clifton, from the spire of whose church
they surveyed the city. The church stands on a hill,
which was such an obvious spot for the enemy to choose
as a site for a battery, that Rupert left a strong force
to hold it and forestall them.

On the 24th, Rupert's formal summons to surrender
was met with the expected rebuff; the 25th was spent in
making final plans and one or two probing attacks to
test the defences; on the 26th the real assault was to go
in at dawn. Rupert had decided, with the support of
his Council of War, to attack from two sides—a difficult
operation throughout the history of warfare until the
introduction of wireless. He had been at some pains to
co-ordinate the two attacks, giving " Oxford " as a pass-
word, and ordering all soldiers to wear green colours
and to fight with bare necks so that they could recognise
each other. Despite his precautions, Maurice's Cornish-
men attacked too soon, at three in the morning, before
Rupert's troops were ready. When Rupert heard the
sounds of firing, and saw the flashes in the air, he tried to
put forward the time of his own attack—another dangerous practice—and his men went in piece-meal. Their
immediate commander, the fiery young Lord Grandison

who had been with Rupert and Maurice at Breda, was mortally wounded in his second attempt to storm the defences; and when his men were ordered to another part of the front they tried to pull out altogether—yet another occurrence not unknown in modern warfare. Rupert himself took command of them, and after having his horse shot under him he managed to effect a lodgment. On the principle of reinforcing success he switched some of Maurice's men to his own side; and early in the afternoon the Roundhead commander, Colonel Fiennes, asked for terms.

Next morning the garrison marched out. They had been promised all honours by Rupert; but they had made the Royalists pay dearly for their victory, and some of Rupert's men, less chivalrous than their commander, failed to abide by his terms, and tried to plunder the vanquished. The two Princes rode in among them belabouring them with their swords, and an eye-witness wrote of Rupert that "some of them felt how sharp his sword was." Rupert apologised to Fiennes; and Fiennes for his part, although in bad odour with the Parliament for his defeat, went out of his way to make known the part played by the Princes in this affair. Roundhead propagandists alleged that the Princes sat their horses and laughed at the excesses of their men; Fiennes denied it. He was not himself the luckiest of officers; he had been among those routed at Powicke Bridge; but he had put up a stout defence of Bristol, and one of Rupert's own officers wrote that "this weak town was so well defended that we wondered why Colonel Fiennes should be banished." The fact that one of Rupert's own officers described the town of Bristol as weak is significant in view of what happened later.

But an unhappy period was at hand. At Bristol Maurice was technically under the command of Lord Hertford; but the two Princes, finding themselves together, had run the battle happily by themselves, and had not done Lord Hertford the courtesy of consulting him about the terms of the surrender. Now, to assert his rights, Hertford appointed Sir Ralph Hopton to be Governor of the city. Rupert had nothing against Hopton, who was an old friend of himself and his family; but Hertford and Maurice (who had been wished on to him as his lieutenant against his will) had been at loggerheads, and Rupert was all for Maurice. Without telling the King that Hertford had appointed Hopton, he asked Charles to give the Governorship to himself; Charles consented, and Rupert appointed Hopton as Lieutenant-Governor. It was a cheap trick, which annoyed many others besides Hertford; and to make matters worse Rupert also induced Charles to make Maurice a General in his own right, an appointment far above his capacity.

Worse was to follow, for a cloud had come over the old, easy friendship with Henrietta Maria. Whether she was jealous of Rupert's ascendancy over the King, or whether she still resented his refusal to join her Church, or whether she was got at by Rupert's enemies in Oxford, or whether—which is probable—it was a combination of all these things, she now ranged herself with all her power against him. He was no longer merely a good-looking and engaging youth, a potential convert to her Church: the King's favourite nephew, a good tennis-player and a hard rider in the hunting-field. He was a major power in this realm of England, and far from amenable at that. He was dangerous. Henceforward the Queen and Rupert were constantly to give the King conflicting advice, and to drive that unhappy man to and fro between them like a shuttlecock. It was a far cry to the days when Rupert was the spoilt darling of the Queen's apartments in Whitehall.

After the capture of Bristol, Maurice returned to the extreme West, which his West-country troops were reluctant to leave. There he contented them by occupying some towns and laying siege to others. The King himself besieged Gloucester, but Essex with a larger army marched to its relief, taking Cirencester and Cheltenham on the way. On Rupert's advice the King raised the siege, and agreed to direct his strategy so as to prevent a junction between Essex's army and another force under Waller which was marching to join him. During this period there is recorded an incident which illustrates how exasperating a master Charles must have been for one of Rupert's temperament. The Prince had spent some hours awaiting orders from the King relating to the pursuit of Essex, knowing that every minute counted. The orders never came, and at last Rupert rode in the darkness to the King's billet. There, looking through the window, he saw the King playing piquet peacefully by the fire with one of his senior officers, while another looked on. He begged him for immediate permission to move, and at last exacted it, despite the protestations of the two generals that the venture was dangerous; he feared that the chance had already passed, and a hard ride through what remained of the night and all the next day brought him to Faringdon, as he thought, too late to intercept. Men and horses were tired out, but, like the good soldier that he was, he did not allow his sympathy for his men to prevail over his tactical instincts; and he sent out mounted patrols for news of Essex. They were commanded by Hurry, that former Roundhead colonel whose information had enabled him to make his successful raid into the Chilterns three months earlier, and luck was with him again: for he brought news that Essex was passing over Aubourne Chase, and hoped to be in Newbury that night. Rupert caught them on the move completely unawares; they reeled back into Hungerford; and time was thus gained for Charles and the main body to arrive and interpose between them and Newbury. It is only fair to Digby and Jermyn, about whom hard things have been and will be said, to record that both of them took part in this long ride, and were wounded in the encounter. In Newbury, as at Wormleighton before Edgehill, Rupert's horsemen found and swallowed up a Roundhead billeting party.

Although it was thus Rupert's accomplishment to have made the first battle of Newbury possible, his counsel for once was on the side of caution. He wanted Charles not to risk a pitched battle, but to go on frittering away Essex's army by harassing and starving it. Possibly he would have accepted as an alternative the making of Newbury into a strong-point. But the King, who had followed Rupert's as against Henrietta Maria's advice on the subject of raising the siege of Gloucester, now took her advice in preference to Rupert's, and resolved to fight west of the town. In giving out his orders, Essex admitted that the Royalists had the best of the position —the hill, the town, the hedges, the River Kennet; but fortunately for him the Royalists failed to hold part of the hill. On the morning of the 20th September, the armies faced each other on the meadows south of the Kennet, while the high ground south of the meadows was divided between the two. On this high ground took place the bitterest fighting. Here the Prince scattered some Roundhead horse; but the trained bands, once more under Skippon, stood fast: Rupert's charge could make no impression on them. The unfamiliar at Edgehill was no longer strange at Newbury: for troops who had had time to take up their positions properly, who knew what to expect, and who were prepared to withstand an onslaught, the new cavalry tactics had lost their terror.

By nightfall the casualties on both sides had been heavy. Rupert himself had had a narrow escape from Sir Philip Stapleton, whose regiment he had chased off the field at Edgehill. Stapleton had ridden up, coolly and alone, to a group of officers among whom Rupert was standing, identified him deliberately, loosed off a pistol at him, and ridden off untouched. Lord Falkland, as honoured a Cavalier as Hampden a Roundhead, had been mortally wounded on a reconnaissance. His monument still stands on the field. The Royalists had expended so much of their precious powder and shot that they could only return one round for every three fired at them. At night they broke off, and early in the morning were on their way to Oxford, while Essex renewed his march towards Reading. But he had not yet finished with Rupert, who pursued him and laid an ambush for his vanguard as it entered Aldermaston. It could have no possible bearing on the course of the war, but it was a neat little piece of cavalry action, and no doubt he got some savage satisfaction for the reverse of the previous day.

Rupert's advice in this campaign had proved to be sound, and his own part in it brilliant, but the Queen's party was nevertheless in the ascendant. His true friends about the Court might stand by him, but the purse-strings and the armouries were not in their gift. Some of the officers in the field with Rupert were also Queen's men; and more than once his own garrisons, which he had carefully sited in key positions, were ordered elsewhere, on some arbitrary mission, direct from Oxford and without reference to him.

Rupert himself had grown wiser, more mature, though not less hot-tempered, with the experience which he had amassed during the past year. Shortly before Newbury, for instance, three Parliamentary lords had come to reconcile themselves to the King: it was Rupert, sensible despite the clash of his various moods, who persuaded Charles to see and forgive them, to the fury of the Queen who wished them spurned. But whenever he rode out of Oxford for long hours in the saddle on the King's business, tongues wagged against him despite the loyal efforts of Richmond, Nicholas, and—when he was not at Rupert's side—Legge. Jermyn was not always ill-disposed to him, but he was not prepared to champion him against the Queen in his absence.

During the autumn and early winter he retook and occupied Bedford and Newport Pagnell. These last two towns, too far distant from Oxford to be closely under his influence, sealed off London from the north, and if strongly held could have proved real thorns in the Parliament's flesh; but the garrison of Newport Pagnell was one of those which was suddenly whisked away on orders from Oxford, and Essex hastily put in a garrison of his own. From all sides Rupert's subordinate commanders complained that they could get neither money nor munitions for their men. The officer in command at Wallingford wrote in December 1643 deploring his lack of strength, and followed it up in January by a request to be relieved of his post, saying: " I would much rather be hanged than be Governor of this place when it is lost." That faded letter recalls something of the difficulties of being a Royalist commander during the fateful winter of 1643-44.

The Prince had a narrow escape in January 1644. False and, as we should call it "planted", information reached him that Aylesbury was willing to declare for the King; and Rupert rode there in a snowstorm. Some instinct or misgiving put him on his guard, and he sent a message into the town from outside asking that the Governor should send out his brother for a parley before he entered. The Governor sent instead a youth, who admitted under pressure that the whole thing was a hoax. Rupert rode back to Thame, sending on to Oxford under arrest the man who had brought the original message, whom he wished to be hanged; but Digby procured his pardon. Was Digby perhaps privy to the plot?

A month later Rupert was off to the north on a new expedition and with a new task: to encourage the Welsh in the King's support, and to strengthen the northern garrisons against the threat of a Scottish army, now preparing to move to the support of Parliament. He had just been created Duke of Cumberland—" Plunderland," said the Roundheads—in order to give him a seat in the Lords; now he was also appointed President of Wales, to give him standing in the Principality. He left at the beginning of February, moving first to Shrewsbury, where he set up some sort of headquarters to deal with Welsh matters. From all quarters of the North were coming requests for help. Newcastle reported that the Scottish army, confronting the town from which he took his title, was fifteen thousand strong; Lord Derby begged for help to his besieged house of Lathom; a Royalist force lately landed from Ireland had been heavily defeated at Nantwich, and needed succour; Newark was also under siege, and in a bad way. At the same time the Parliamentary garrisons north of Birmingham were deafening Essex with requests for help because Rupert and his " caniballs " were upon them. Rupert decided that the relief of Newark must be his first task. The besiegers under Sir John Meldrum outnumbered his own force, but he managed to pass an uncompromising written message to Sir John Henderson, commanding the castle, saying: " Let the old Drum be beaten early on the morrow morning." Henderson had the wit to discern the hidden meaning, and made a sortie before dawn, joining hands with Rupert while Meldrum still believed him to be several miles away. The enemy were thrust back into their own defences, during an action in which Rupert, fighting hand to hand, was rescued at an awkward moment by Sir Richard Crane, his old companion of Vlotho. In the evening another of Rupert's officers, who had been captured early in the day, brought a request for terms from Meldrum; and Rupert found himself the richer by several thousand muskets, eleven guns, fifty barrels of powder and other useful trophies. This was a hearty little affair in the best Rupert tradition.

He was not immediately strong enough to push on northward, until he could recruit more levies; and when at last he was ready to proceed, he was summoned back, to his great disgust, to Oxford. He went in an impatient mood, and succeeded in making the King agree to his plans: that the King should stay in Oxford, maintaining just such cavalry activity as Rupert had carried out during the previous year; that Maurice should carry on in the West, and that he himself should be left free for his ploys in the North. But Rupert was not twenty-four hours gone from Oxford before the King was persuaded by contrary counsel from the egregious Digby. Later on the remorseful Charles was to write to Rupert:

I believe that if you had been with me I had not been put to the straits I am in now. I confess the best had been to have followed your advice.

But the mischief was done: Reading and Abingdon

R.R.   E were abandoned, and the King was soon manœuvred out of Oxford itself, which under Rupert's wise dispositions had never been seriously threatened since it was first occupied twenty months before. Leaving a small garrison, the King set off upon a circuitous march, harassed by Waller, to Evesham, Worcester, Evesham again, Witney, and so to Cropredy near Banbury, where more by good luck than good management he captured the whole of Waller's artillery, and won himself a breathing space. He then set off for Exeter, where the Queen had gone some time before for the birth of Princess Henrietta, her last child; but she had been obliged by the threat of Essex's approach to take ship for France. She and the King were never to meet again, nor was the King ever to see his youngest daughter.

Meanwhile Rupert was having his last run of success. He occupied Nantwich on the 18th of May; and his coming must have inspired some fear: it was known that, for thirteen Irish prisoners hanged there a few weeks earlier, on the grounds that they had no business to be fighting for the King in England, he had hanged thirteen Roundhead prisoners on the principle of an eye for an eye. On the 20th he was at Chester, of which he made Will Legge the Governor. On the 23rd he took Knutsford, and on the 25th Stockport. On hearing this news, the besiegers of Lathom, which had been gallantly defended for three months by Lord Derby's French wife, retired to Bolton. The Prince, in whose army Derby himself was riding, had no knowledge of this when he decided to make for Bolton himself. This town was the pride of the Puritans, who liked to call it " the Geneva of the North."

The fighting in Bolton was the bitterest of the war; the defenders were fanatical, and the blood of the attackers was up. The Cavaliers had been twice repulsed when the defenders hung a prisoner over the walls as a sign of defiance. This was too much for Rupert. As at Brentford, he leapt off his horse, put himself at the head of a foot regiment and led a new charge. That was the beginning of the end, and there was a horrible slaughter, which did not cease with the surrender of the garrison. Lord Derby himself encountered one Booth, who had been brought up as his wife's protégé at Lathom, and who had deserted to the enemy in the middle of the siege with all the information about the defence that he could collect; and Derby took the greatest possible pleasure in running Booth through with his sword.

Wigan, where Rupert had a triumphant entry, and Liverpool were next secured; but the quantities of stores which he had hoped to find at the latter had all been evacuated by sea. He ordered the Bishop of Chester to collect money for the relief of his wounded, and to cause all the clergy in his diocese to exhort their parishes to be loyal to the King. A week's fighting had won him Lancashire, downcast the Parliament, and given new heart to Lord Newcastle and the sorely pressed defenders of York, who were near the end of their tether. A well-informed Norfolk squire,[1] writing to his home from London on the 12th of June, thus sums the matter up:

[1] . . . Knyvett. *The Knyvett Papers*, ed. Dr. B. Schofield, London, 1949.

They say Prince Rupert is swelled into a huge army in Lancashire. The taking of York continues yet dubious, though reputed here in great distress. The Lord Manchester's men behave themselves gallantly. If Prince Rupert comes into the relief they may perhaps hold out a little longer; but my Lord of Manchester and the Scots are two numerous armies to be dealt with, and Prince Rupert may have his hands full if he comes near them.

Goring with seven thousand men was awaiting Rupert in the West Riding of Yorkshire. A frantic letter from the King, dated from Buckingham on the 22nd of June, a week before Cropredy, asked for the services of Goring with all speed, " as you love your own preservation and mine." But Rupert had already received from the same source a far more weighty letter dated the 14th of June, a letter to which he attached so much importance that he carried it with him for the rest of his life. It provided the answer to those of his enemies who said that he should never have fought the battle of Marston Moor.

It opens with congratulations on his successes, and goes on:

Now that I must give the true state of my affairs, which, if their condition be such as enforces me to give you more peremptory commands than I would willingly do, you must not take it ill. If York be lost I shall esteem my crown little less[1]; unless supported by your sudden march to me, and a miraculous

[1] *I.e.* I shall pretty well have lost my crown too.

conquest in the South, before the effects of the Northern power can be felt here. But if York be relieved, and you beat the rebels' armies of both kingdoms, which are before it, then (but otherwise not[1]) I may possibly make a shift upon the defensive to spin out time until you come to assist me. Wherefore I command and conjure you, by all the duty and affection which I know you bear me, that, all enterprises laid aside, you immediately march, according to your first intention, with all your force to the relief of York. . . . You may believe that nothing but an extreme necessity could make me write thus unto you; wherefore in this case I can no ways doubt of your punctual compliance with

Your loving and most faithful friend,
Charles R.

In fairness to King Charles it should be remembered that this letter was written while he was on the run, doubling back from Worcester to Evesham while Waller chased him; but in fairness to Rupert it must be declared that he could hardly have received more precise orders. One courtier, no friend to him, saw a copy of the letter after its despatch; and having confirmed from the King that it had actually gone, " Why then," he said, " before God you are undone, for upon this peremptory order he will fight, whatever comes on't."

It must have been tempting to wait a little longer so

---

[1] The words in parentheses are said to have been added on the advice of Wilmot.

as to raise more levies out of loyal Wales, to which he
was so near; but this letter, coupled with the entreaties
of Lord Newcastle and the garrison of York, made it
imperative that he should move at once. He went by
Denton, Skipton and the Aire Valley to Knaresborough; at Denton, the family home of the Fairfaxes,
now in the field against him, he saw the portraits of other
Fairfaxes who had been killed fighting for his father's
fortunes in the Palatinate, and saw to it that the house
was treated with respect and honour. On the 1st of
July they passed through Knaresborough, and were led
by Goring, who knew the country, round the Parliamentarian flank to the north. With two thousand cavalry
Rupert rode into York, and met Newcastle, who, in the
hastily assembled Council of War, advised Rupert to
avoid battle. The Prince replied, " Nothing venture,
nothing have," and assured him that he had positive
orders to fight. He passed straight out of York towards
Marston Moor, bidding Newcastle follow as soon as he
could muster his men. The Parliamentarian and Scots
armies were for the moment some miles apart, and with
a little of his old luck Rupert might have defeated the
English at Marston before the Scots could join them
from Tadcaster, three or four miles to the south. But
the chance, if chance it was, quickly passed, and he was
obliged to fight the joint enemy at their full strength.

Something like a curse lay upon Rupert at Marston
Moor. His style does not ring quite true; there were
inauspicious incidents. The weight of the King's letter
was on his mind. His new-found colleague, Newcastle, had no stomach for the fight. James King,

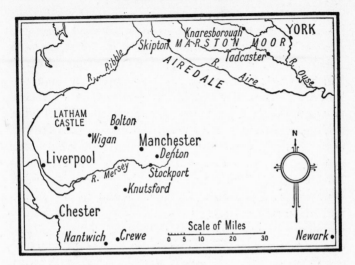

now Lord Eythin, the evil genius of Vlotho six years before, was among Newcastle's advisers: what could be a worse augury for an anxious young general, about to fight a critical battle? Rupert showed King his plan, and King sneered at it; he offered to amend it, and King said it was too late. He heard that Cromwell, whom he had never fought before, was among those ranged against him: he sent him a foolish, mocking message, and got a confident rejoinder. To crown all, and apart from fancies, there remained the hard fact that he was outnumbered in the ratio of three to two.

The two armies were face to face by 7 pm., on the night of the 2nd July. Rupert had drawn up his line with his own horse, under Sir John Byron, on the right; Newcastle's infantry were in the centre; and Goring, whose conduct on this day was beyond reproach, was marshalling his horse on the left. Cromwell faced Byron; English and Scottish infantry, from west to east, had the centre; Sir Thomas Fairfax opposed Goring. Rupert and Newcastle both seem to have assumed that the battle would not begin that night, for Newcastle was smoking in his six-horsed coach and Rupert was supping when first the Roundhead and then the Royalist guns opened fire. A heavy thunderstorm broke as the armies met, deluging the battlefield with rain and hail. On the Royalist right Byron had an initial success in which Cromwell was wounded, but soon found himself being pushed back; it was to this flank that Rupert rushed, but after a short spell of hard fighting it went against him. On the other flank it was the Roundheads who had the first success, and Goring who at last had the best of it: the whole battle was swinging clockwise. But it was in the centre and on the Royalist right that the issue was decided. Newcastle's white-coated infantry, weak, perhaps, from the privations of their long siege, stood their ground to be cut to pieces almost to a man: only thirty survived. The battle was over in an hour, and the Cavaliers were fleeing in confusion.

Rupert himself had had to put his horse at a fence to make good his retreat. He found himself in a bean-field, and set to work to rally what was left of his men. Collecting the equivalent of a few squadrons, he rode towards York, chose a good position in some enclosed country, lined the hedges and beat off his pursuers under Cromwell, who had had his wound dressed and returned to the field. Soon he fell in with Newcastle

and King; and a contemporary account has preserved
their talk:

Says General King, " What will you do? "
Says the Prince, " I will rally my men."
Says General King, " Now you, Lord Newcastle, what
  will you do? "
Says Lord Newcastle, " I will go into Holland."
The Prince would have him endeavour to recruit his
  forces.
" No," says he, " I will not endure the laughter of
  the Court."

So Newcastle fled, not to Holland but to Hamburg,
in a fishing boat from Scarborough; and King went with
him, and suffered the bitter reproaches of the Prince,
which stung him into writing a letter in protest; and
Rupert was as good as his word and his character,
rallying such men as he could and withdrawing to the
north and west, and so down to the Welsh Marches. As
he went, two days after the battle, he met for the first
and apparently the only time James Graham, Marquis
of Montrose, who had been on his way to join him: they
spent a night together at Richmond, forty miles north-
west of York, but there is no record of the talk that
passed between the two most romantic figures of their
time. Next morning Rupert went his way westward,
and Montrose, who was almost unaccompanied, returned
towards Scotland.

At Marston Moor Rupert lost both his army and his
reputation, however unjustly. And as though Fate had

not already dealt him blows enough in a couple of evening hours, he had lost his beloved dog as well. Boy had been with him as he was eating his supper, he had followed him in the first charge, and his carcase was discovered by exulting Roundheads as they went about burying the dead.

* 4 *

Naseby

THE SUPPORTERS of the Parliament could scarcely believe in the magnitude of the victory at Marston Moor. Knyvett, the Norfolk squire already quoted, wrote on the 11th July, nine days after the battle:

> We hope here that the North will be quiet in a short time, but that this troublesome Prince may chance to make head again. We fear he hath got together a shrewd party of his horse.

Ludlow, the Regicide, writing long afterwards but always in ignorance of the King's letter, was still speculating as to why the battle had been fought at all:

> If Prince Rupert, who had acquired honour enough by the relief of York in the view of three generals, could have contented himself with it, and retreated, as he might have done, without fighting, the reputation he had gained would have caused his army to increase like the rolling of a snowball; but he, thinking this nothing unless he might have all, forced his enemies

to a battle against the advice of many of those who were with him.

Rupert at any rate was under no illusions as he rode over into Lancashire with six thousand of his horse. The signs of lost confidence which were present in his manner just before the battle are equally evident in his conduct after it. Although his conscience was clear that in the light of the King's orders he had no option but to fight the battle, he may well have asked himself whether he had fought it with all his old skill. There are grounds for belief that he had failed to reconnoitre the ground with his usual thoroughness. He despised Newcastle and King for running away to the Continent rather than face the Court; yet he himself could not face the King. For two months he lingered in Lancashire and Cheshire, and upon the Welsh Marches, raising levies, and according to some accounts, giving way to dissipations such as he had often despised in others. Goring, on the other hand, who alone on the Royalist side could boast of his part at Marston Moor—except for Newcastle's infantry, and they were dead—went straight to the King in Cornwall to bask in the favours of the Court. He chose his moment well: for Wilmot had just been discovered in private— there is little reason to shirk the word " treasonable "— correspondence with Essex. He was arrested, and his command as General of the Horse was given to Goring, who had arrived at the peripatetic court the night before. It was not a happy command, for the officers preferred Wilmot to Goring, and forty-four of the more senior addressed a respectful message to Charles asking for clemency for their former commander. Goring wrote to Rupert, saying that he had never seen a more mutinous army, and expressing the hope that when the current crisis was over he might serve once more under the Prince. All the same, the army of the West had a success at the beginning of September, when it cornered Essex at Lostwithiel in the Fowey peninsula. Essex himself escaped with some of his officers in a small boat; the cavalry under Balfour broke out while Goring was engaged in a debauch; the infantry under Skippon was allowed to march away on the usual chivalrous terms, having surrendered arms and ammunition.

The supersession of Wilmot by Goring had been so unpopular that the King sought to sugar the pill by saying that Rupert approved. Probably he would have, since he had no love for Wilmot; but in actual fact he had not been consulted; and the announcement did not endear him to Wilmot nor to Wilmot's former officers. Wilmot had gone to the Continent, where he fell in with Newcastle, and each vied with the other in retailing their grievances, finding a ready listener in Henrietta Maria.

Rupert met the King at last in Lord Poulett's house at Crewkerne, on the Somerset-Dorset border, at the end of September, nearly three months after Marston Moor. Rupert was in poor form, as had been reported: haunted by his defeat, disturbed by the encouragement it had given to his enemies, worried by news from Legge that things were going ill in Lancashire, and heartened only by a kindly and tactful letter from his friend the Duke of Richmond, making it clear that the Duke, at any rate, looked to Rupert alone to pull the tattered cause together.

At Crewkerne, however, he recovered himself and produced a new plan for the King. The remnants of the northern army were to be brought south; Bristol was to be put into a state of defence; no further engagement was to be sought until the army was trained and ready for it. The King agreed; and on that understanding they parted, the King towards Oxford, Rupert to Bristol. But the King was tempted into the second battle of Newbury by Goring's optimism and by his own wish to raise the sieges of several Royalist garrisons; and once again suffered the worst of an inconclusive fight. The King seems to have persuaded himself that if Rupert had been present all would have been well; and early in November, two years too late, he at last nominated Rupert to be General-in-Chief in place of Ruthven, who was old and deaf and, according to Chancellor Hyde, " dozed in his understanding " through drink.

It was two years too late; and Rupert realised it only too well. Even Abingdon, barely six miles from Oxford, which had long been the base from which his cavalry in its heyday had made its classic raids, was now so firmly in Roundhead hands that he could not recapture it. Many of the best of the Cavaliers had long since fallen. Montrose was at large with his army, but in Scotland, and much too far away to influence affairs in England. With Digby and Goring Rupert had an uneasy truce. Of Digby he wrote to Legge: " Rupert and Digby are friends, but I doubt they trust one another alike ! " Of Goring, Rupert's secretary wrote similarly: " Goring and Prince Rupert are now friends, but I doubt the building being made of green wood, which is apt to warp and yield." And the King, as though afraid that in making Rupert General-in-Chief he had gone too far, now made two appointments of which the Prince could not possibly approve. Goring was made an independent commander, with the right of receiving his orders direct from Charles, just as Rupert had been made independent on his first arrival in 1642; and Lord Bernard Stuart was given the Colonelcy of the Life Guards, which Rupert considered his own perquisite. Goring could not resist crowing over his triumph in a letter to Rupert, which must have stung him the more because he remembered his own former satisfaction. Lord Bernard's appointment riled the Prince so much that he asked for his passport back to Holland. It was probably the Duke of Richmond, Lord Bernard's brother, who persuaded him not to insist: for of all of his acquaintance there were only three whose advice he never spurned, and whose friendship towards him never wavered, Richmond and his pretty wife, and " Honest Will " Legge. But the friendship with Goring was already " warped," and from now on we find extreme coolness in Rupert's communications with him. " I shall desire your Lordship . . . I shall expect your Lordship . . ." He could desire, and he could expect; but he could not command.

Rupert was a realist now. In contrast to that earlier Rupert who had been so impatient with the peace party about the King, he supported the new negotiations for peace which opened at the end of the year. Richmond was sent by Charles to make overtures at Uxbridge in December; but they were doomed from the start. Apart from the garrisons about Oxford, and Montrose far away

in Scotland, the King had no armies left in the field but
that of Goring in the West. Cromwell's New Model
Army was growing every day, and Parliament felt strong
enough to lay down its own conditions. These included
a long list of names to whom no pardon would be ex-
tended. Those of Rupert and Maurice were both
mentioned, and when these were read out at Court they
both burst into such loud and boisterous laughter that
the King himself told them to be quiet. It was while
talks were actually in progress that the Parliament put
an end to them by the execution of Archbishop Laud,
who had been a prisoner in their hands since the
beginning of the war.

The New Year began badly. In the West, the peasants
were rising in despair at the exactions of both sides, and
the collection of supplies was becoming more and more
difficult. Of the fortresses covering the two main roads
into Wales, Shrewsbury was lost through treachery and
Cirencester was on the verge of mutiny for lack of pay
and warlike stores. A plot for the surrender of Newark
was discovered and suppressed in the nick of time.
Rupert set off from Oxford at the beginning of March
to see what he could do to put matters right. His
depression fell from him as he found himself in the field,
and he had two or three small successes in Gloucestershire
and Shropshire, due to rapid marches and swift
strikes. He returned to Oxford at the beginning of May
with some new Welsh levies, to find that Cromwell had
captured Bletchingdon, as close to Oxford on the north
as Abingdon, already lost, upon the south. The unfortunate Governor of Bletchingdon had already been

executed, a plea for Rupert's intervention having fallen into Roundhead hands.

A conference to decide future policy was held at Woodstock. There was little to be cheerful about. The only glimmers of comfort in a sombre scene were the recent successes of Montrose in Scotland, and some reliable reports of friction between the Parliament and their Scottish allies. The northern horsemen in the King's army were anxious to serve him nearer their own homes. The feeling of the Council was that more was to be gained in a campaign towards the north than by sitting in the straitened defences of Oxford; and the following decisions were taken. Goring was to continue in command in the West. Bristol was to be defended under the nominal command of the Prince of Wales who was aged only fourteen, with Richmond and Hopton to advise him. Legge was to hold Oxford with an adequate garrison. The main army, with the King and Rupert, was to go North.

The King, his nephew and the Royal Army, small as it was, moved slowly by Chipping Norton, Evesham, Bromsgrove, Wolverhampton, and so eastward by Ashby-de-la-Zouch to Leicester, where, on the scene of his first indiscretion, Rupert was to win the King his last success. After twenty-four hours of preparation he breached the walls with artillery, and then assaulted them. The garrison fought desperately, setting up barricades of woolpacks, the staple product from which the town had won its fame and wealth: half the day and most of the night were needed to reduce them; fighting proceeded from house to house. Leicester was a real prize, for it was a rich town and full of the sinews of war; but its capture was not the prelude to a new series of victories. Once again the King suffered his mind to be made up for him by Digby, and turned back towards Oxford.

It is not impossible that Fairfax and Cromwell had intensified their pressure on Oxford with the very object of luring the King's army back again in that direction. The young Duke of York and many ladies of the Court had been left in the city, and were become hostages to fortune; in the light of the new threat, Legge's garrison no longer seemed as adequate as it had appeared to be at the council-table of Woodstock. Yet, when the King's army had reached Daventry, fifty miles short of Oxford, they heard that Fairfax had broken off the siege and was moving towards them. Rupert advised a withdrawal to the north, Digby a battle. The King postponed his decision, and events took their fated course.

The King was spending the night of the 13th of June at Lubenham, two miles west of Market Harborough, where Rupert and his cavalry lay.[1] Rupert had set an outpost at Naseby, six miles to the south along the Oxford road; but the men of the outpost were easy-going soldiers, far from on the alert. They were playing quoits when they were surprised by Roundhead cavalry under Ireton—the table on which their tankards were standing may be seen to this day in Naseby Church. Only one man escaped: he mounted and galloped to Lubenham. The King was awakened, and he too got to horse and rode to Rupert. The Prince was still convinced that the proper course was to move on northwards,

[1] See map on page 37.

where additional troops at Melton Mowbray and Newark were awaiting their arrival, but he was overruled by the King. The soldiers were already standing to, and soon after first light they were drawn up on a ridge a couple of miles south of Market Harborough, under Sir Jacob Astley. Astley was forty years older than Rupert and had known him since he was a child; but he had never once questioned his orders, and he had as stout a heart and upright a character as any man of his day and age.

At first Rupert's scouts failed to find the enemy, and he made a reconnaissance himself. He found that if he stayed where he was boggy ground would intervene between him and the enemy, giving him no scope for his main asset, the cavalry. As he rode forward he saw the enemy moving westward. Perhaps he thought they were withdrawing; perhaps he thought they were trying to get to windward of him, an important advantage in those days of black powder. Whatever his reasons, he moved the whole of the royal army including Astley to high ground which lay forward and to the right, nearly two miles beyond the position which Astley had provisionally taken up. To the east of this high ground the streams run down to find their way into the North Sea; those to the west flow at last into the Avon and the Bristol Channel. And so it was that this battle, which was to decide the Civil War, was fought in the very middle of England.

Rupert might have been wiser to await the enemy's attack in Astley's position. The Roundhead army was exactly twice the size of the King's; it had been reinforced, unknown to Rupert, during the night. But there was no certainty that the enemy would attack there: he might await a better moment, or use his greater strength to turn the flank. Rupert had never fought a defensive battle, and all his successes had sprung from attacking. To-day he would attack.

Between nine and ten in the morning, Astley advanced against the Roundhead infantry under Skippon, and Rupert charged their left under Ireton. For the last time in his career he saw his enemies break before him and pursued them off the field. The Royalist infantry did well at first; Skippon was badly wounded and his men gave ground. But Rupert, charging up a gentle slope, left some of Ireton's horse untouched; and he did not know that some more horse under Colonel Okey had been concealed behind hedges some hundreds of yards to his right flank. When Rupert had gone past, chasing the greater part of Ireton's men into Naseby village, and beating up the Parliamentary baggage-train, Okey and the remnant of Ireton's horse charged into Astley's right flank. From the other side of the field, Cromwell, having thrown back the Royalist left in disorder and sent a detachment to prevent their return to the battle, now closed in himself to complete the iron ring round Astley's infantry.

The superior strength of the Roundheads was telling. The Royalists had one hope left; if they threw in their reserves with enough vigour they might still win. The King seems to have realised this, for he formed up his remaining cavalry crying: " One charge more, and the day is ours! " At that moment Lord Carnwath said to him: " Will you go to your death? " seized his bridle, turned his horse's head and led him off the field. Better, perhaps, if Charles had indeed gone to his death that day, instead of meeting it on the scaffold four unhappy years later. The news spread quickly, and the battle was over. Only a few devoted infantrymen fought it out, and the King is said to have watched their end from a few hundred yards away. Then he rode to Ashby-de-la-Zouch, while Cromwell's horse pursued the fugitives to the gates of Leicester, and lesser men put to death three hundred Royalist wives and other camp-followers whom they found abandoned. Half the Royalist army was killed or taken; all the colours, all the baggage, all the treasure, all the King's correspondence, including all his private letters from his wife and children. Never was there a more utter defeat.

At Ashby the King and Rupert parted company. Rupert went to Bristol, the King by Lichfield and Hereford to Ragland, where the aged Marquis of Worcester, a Catholic who had spent close on a million pounds in his cause, entertained him with a lavishness such as he had never known. There he spent three weeks, while the Roundheads mopped up disheartened garrisons all over England from Carlisle to Bridgwater, and defeated his last field army under Goring at Langport in Somerset. He met Rupert in conference at Cardiff, and then set off on interminable and fruitless journeys up and down the kingdom which he could no longer hope to regain.

* 5 *

The Doomed Cause

RUPERT inevitably got the blame of Naseby. He knew he would; he said so in a letter which he wrote to Legge just after the battle. The King had once again turned to Digby who had advised fighting at Naseby when Rupert was advocating caution, Digby whose advice was behind the fateful letter which had precipitated Marston Moor. Legge now received a letter from Digby as well as from Rupert, an ingenious letter which, while it protested his affection for Rupert, hinted in every line that Rupert was to blame for the disaster, and suggesting that the root cause of the trouble had been the absence of Legge's own wise counsel from Rupert's side. This was too much for " Honest Will," who sat down and wrote a reply which can have left Digby in no doubt of his views, and of which the bluff sincerity rings true across three centuries:

Your last letter gives me cause to think that your Lordship is not altogether free from what His Highness accused you of, which was that you both say and do things to his prejudice, contrary to your professions, and not in an open and direct line, but obscurely and obliquely; and this, under your Lordship's pardon,

I find your letter very full of. For my part, my Lord, I am so well acquainted with the Prince's ways, that I am confident all his General officers and commanders knew beforehand how and in what manner he intended to fight. . . . Assure yourself your are not free from great blame towards Prince Rupert. And no man will give you this free language at a cheaper rate than myself, though many discourse of it.

A few days after Digby received this rebuke, he was writing to Jermyn, rejoicing at the King's resolution in future to restrict Rupert to " action," and to exclude him " from counsel and debate, which, could it have been sooner obtained, we should not have been now put to such an unhappy after-game." Unfortunately for his standing with posterity, he dated it on the very day of Goring's defeat at Langport. Rupert was busily engaged in preparing for the " action " which he knew must soon come to him at Bristol, but he still had one piece of " counsel " for the King, and nothing would stop him giving it: the wisdom of it was obvious. Whether or not it would give offence, he was determined to do his duty and to speak his mind freely: the King must sue for peace.

Charles's answer was delayed, but when it arrived it was firm. He realised that Rupert had meant well, but he must not proffer such advice again. However bad the situation might look to the eye of a mere soldier or statesman, speaking as a Christian, he knew that God would not suffer his cause to be overthrown.

Rupert had done his duty in counsel and been rebuffed; now he devoted all his attention to preparing Bristol for a siege. At the end of July he wrote to Will Legge, who had heard disquieting rumours about the state of its defences, that he was surprised that he should have heard so many false tales, and that they were never in better case. He told the King that he could hold it for four months. But unfortunately Legge's information was correct; and in the light of after events it is hard to see why Rupert should have been so sanguine, not only to the King, but also to his more intimate friend, in whom one would have expected him to confide freely. The perimeter which had to be defended was five miles round, the breastworks were nowhere more than five feet high nor the ditch than five feet deep. The garrison at most was 2,300, including many raw Welshmen and eight hundred ill-trained and discontented auxiliaries from the town. The fort had no water-supply and was commanded by higher ground which the Prince could not afford to hold for lack of numbers. And finally the population was riddled with Roundhead agents, spreading disaffection and treachery.

Fairfax commanded the besiegers, and summoned Rupert to surrender in unusual terms:

I take into consideration your Royal birth, and relation to the Crown of England, your honour, courage, and the virtue of your person, and the strength of that place which you may think yourself bound and able to maintain. Sir, the Crown of England is and will be where it ought to be, we fight to maintain it there . . . To maintain the rights of the Crown of England jointly, a principal part whereof is that the

King in supreme acts concerning the whole State is not to be advised by men of whom the law takes no notice, but by his Parliament,—the great Council of the Kingdom. . . .

Sir, if God makes this clear to you as he has to us, I doubt not but he will give you a heart to deliver this place. . . . And if upon such conviction you should surrender it, and save the loss of blood or hazard of spoiling such a city, it would be an occasion glorious to us, for the restoring of you to the endeared affection of the Parliament and people of England— the truest friends to your family that it hath in the world. . . . And let all England judge. . . .

To this not unworthy appeal, with its assurances concerning the Crown, the signature of Cromwell is not to be found, though he signed jointly with Fairfax another paper promising protection to the citizens if they did not resist. The debt of Rupert's family to that of Fairfax was no light one, and Rupert, knowing the hopeless odds against him, and remembering his own counsel to the King, may well have been touched by it; but he only replied by asking time to refer the terms to the King, which Fairfax refused. The Prince still delayed, and worked desperately at improving his miserable defences, while keeping Fairfax at bay. In one of the preliminary skirmishes, Rupert's old friend Sir Richard Crane was killed. At last Fairfax's patience was finished, and he assaulted at two in the morning of the 10th of September. The first brunt fell on the auxiliaries and " new Welsh," and in a short time the defenders were

separated from each other and divided up into smaller
groups. By dawn they were in such a bad way that the
Prince asked for terms, and received honourable ones.
The garrison was to march out with colours, pikes and
drums, bag and baggage, horses and swords; and the
Prince's own life-guards were to retain their weapons,
as were all the officers. They were to be given eight
days to reach any garrison of the King which the Prince
might name, so long as it was more than fifty miles
from Bristol.

On the 11th of September the garrison marched out.
The Prince's cavalry was drawn up on the green below
the fort, with eight wagons of baggage. By the gate of
the fort stood Cromwell with a group of Roundhead
officers, and Colonel Hammond, waiting to receive the
keys at the head of his regiment. Then from the gate
came the leading half of Rupert's escort of Life Guards,
gorgeous in red tunics and carrying their firelocks. And
then appeared the awaited figure of the defeated Prince,
" clad in scarlet, very richly laid in silver lace, mounted
on a very gallant black Barbary horse," and followed by
the second half of his escort. Cromwell and his companions accompanied the Prince to where Fairfax was
awaiting him. The two met, and the Prince named
Oxford as the garrison to which he chose to go, under
the terms; and Fairfax rode the first two miles with him,
giving him the place of honour on the right, and talking
amicably with him, while three hundred noblemen and
gentlemen of the Prince's party, his two thousand infantry,
his four hundred cavalry and his eight wagons rolled
across Durdham Downs. It is said that the Prince told

Fairfax that he was convinced that the war was over, which may be counted an indiscretion; but he certainly behaved with dignity, and won the admiration of his opponents in his hour of humiliation. He asked for muskets for the journey, to protect his men against the clubmen, undertaking to surrender them when he got to Oxford; and such was their trust in his word that the request was granted.

The Roundhead Colonel Butler, who was deputed to travel with him to Oxford, was so taken with him that he wrote to Waller:

> Seriously, I am glad I had the happiness to see him. I am confident we have been much mistaken in our intelligence concerning him. I find him a man much inclined to a happy peace, and he will certainly employ his interest with His Majesty for the accomplishing of it. I make it my request to you . . . that no pamphlet is printed that may derogate from his worth for the delivery of Bristol. On my word he could not have held it unless it had been better manned.

So much for the regard of his enemies. The outburst from his friends was deafening. Charges of treachery and poltroonery rent the air. The King, ensconced at Ragland, signed a document on the 14th of September divesting Rupert of all military authority whatsoever within his dominions, and requiring all commanders, officers and soldiers to take note of it. He sent Rupert his passport to leave the Kingdom; it was signed, with what pleasure may be guessed, by Digby. He dismissed

Legge from his Governorship of Oxford and put him under arrest, for no better reason than that he was Rupert's friend, and despite the fact that at the time of the disaster at Bristol, he had been in Oxford, eighty miles away, and in no way concerned in the affair at Bristol. He wrote to Maurice a placatory letter—that is to say, it might have been placatory to somebody other than Maurice—absolving him from complicity in Rupert's present " misfortune." And finally he sent a message to the little Duke of York saying that he would rather hear that the said little Duke of York had been knocked on the head than that he should do so mean an action as surrender Bristol.

Legge, who was imprisoned no fewer than eleven times in the course of his career, went into arrest with his usual equanimity. Maurice was sick with fever at Worcester and too ill to travel, but he copied out the King's letter with his own hand, sent it to Rupert and joined him in person as soon as he could, to demonstrate that his first loyalty was to his adored brother rather than to his uncle. Rupert himself wrote a dignified letter to the King, who had sent him a sorrowful but reproachful one along with his passport and dismissal. The core of Rupert's lay in the single sentence: " If your Majesty had vouchsafed me so much patience as to hear me inform you, before you had made a final judgment, you would not have censured me as it seems you do." He asked in moving terms for an interview, scorning to cite his past services beyond reminding his uncle that there had been some.

To this letter he received no reply, and he determined

to go and see the King with or without his permission.
He had neither means nor money with which to leave
the Kingdom, nor a passport from the Parliament, without which he would have difficulty in finding a ship;
but most of all he wished to justify himself in the eyes of
the King and the world, and to bring about Legge's
release from his unjustified imprisonment. The King was
now at Newark, and the country between was swarming
with Roundheads; but to Newark, whatever the dangers,
he was determined to go. And so he set out with a
handful of friends to ride across four counties of England
where both sides were now against him. It was not the
least exciting adventure of his life.

With eighty horsemen, many of them gentlemen, he
rode first to Banbury, where Maurice joined him; thence
to Burghley in Northamptonshire, where the Governor
tried to intercept him. The Governor was a renegade
Cavalier who had long before served under Rupert; he
tried to shoot the Prince with his pistol, cried for quarter
when it missed fire, and was himself shot dead by the
Prince. Rupert's party rode on, but by this time the
Parliament had guessed what he was about, and bands
of cavalry were sent in all directions to try to block his
road. Near Belvoir Castle, which was still for the King,
they came to a bridge which was held by three hundred
Roundhead horsemen: the Prince first made as if to
charge, but then turned and galloped away with the
enemy in full cry behind him. Then he turned and struck
at them as they came, and a few minutes later repeated
the same manœuvre. By now more enemy had arrived,
and the Prince said: " We have beaten them twice, we

must beat them once more, and then over the pass and away."

The Prince now split his party, sending some with his scanty baggage to Belvoir by one route, while he himself with Lord Hawley, Sir William Vavasour (both of whom had been at Bristol with him and considered their honour linked with his own), Prince Maurice and twenty more, proceeded to lead their pursuers a dance. There had come back into the Prince's mind memories of " a particular way, which he had learned ten years before, being at Belvoir Castle . . . hunting and shooting of conies." The party in chase of them was now only forty strong, and the Prince allowed them to catch him up, telling his companions to keep close together and to turn when he turned. The enemy offered them quarter, and then came raggedly down the hill, the Prince and his men turned and beat them fairly and squarely. Lord Molineux killed a man on a better horse than Rupert's; Rupert exchanged horses, " and so, fair and softly, went to Belvoir." There they found that fourteen of the rest of their party had been caught.

At Belvoir also they found a message from the King, forbidding them to come any nearer, and saying that he refused to receive Rupert. To this they paid no attention, but rode on next day the fifteen remaining miles to Newark. Sir Richard Willis, the Governor, came out to meet them a mile or two from the town, and told Rupert that he and many others in the Castle were with him heart and soul. He told him also that Digby was no longer there; he had ridden out with the King a few days before, and the King had returned without him, allowing him to go north to join Montrose with the bulk of the cavalry still remaining. Digby knew that Rupert was on his way to see the King: why did he not stay to face him? We can only guess that the temper of the rest of the Cavaliers at Newark was so plainly for Rupert that Digby feared to await his arrival.

The cavalcade which had dared so many dangers rode into the town, and Rupert went straight into the King's presence, without ceremony, saying that he had come to render an account of the loss of Bristol. The King made no reply, but went to supper. Rupert and Maurice followed him in, and stood beside him while he ate; he made a few remarks to Maurice, but totally ignored Rupert. Then he went to bed, and the Princes to Sir Richard Willis's house.

Next morning, without again seeing the King, Rupert was granted a court martial before seven officers. There was Lindsey, now Lord Great Chamberlain; Lords Cork, Bellasis and Gerrard; Sir Jacob, who had just become Lord, Astley; Willis; and John Ashburnham, the Treasurer-at-War. Of these seven men, to whom Rupert looked to uphold his honour, nothing is known about the affections of Cork; Lindsey's father, as will be remembered, had been killed at Edgehill after and perhaps directly because of his disagreement with Rupert; Willis and Gerrard were old friends of Rupert, and made no secret of it; Astley was a still older friend, but so honourable that he could be trusted to speak his mind on either side without fear or favour; Bellasis was a creature of Digby's, who was afterwards to perish in a drunken brawl in France; Ashburnham was a trimmer and a whisperer, who had sometimes been for Digby and sometimes for Rupert, and had once been described by a friend of Rupert's as " slippery."

Rupert laid before the court martial a narrative of the siege, with statements signed by his engineers and by various of his officers, about the weakness of the garrison and the state of the defences; he also handed in copies of the terms on which he had surrendered. The findings of the first day acquitted him of want of courage or fidelity, but added that he might have held the castle and fort for longer than he did, in view of the Royal intention to send a force to his relief. To this rider Rupert answered that in his decision he had had the support of his Council of War; that he had heard nothing of any project to relieve him; and that so far as his own knowledge went at the time, he could not possibly have expected any such relief. The King's secretary—not Nicholas but another—went on record in his own diary saying, more or less, that he could not for the life of him imagine where such a relief could have come from.

A second hearing was held three days later, on the 21st of October, before the King himself, still supported by the seven officers, to consider these observations of Rupert's. The King then declared, without any rider or reservation, that " Our said right dear nephew, Prince Rupert, is not guilty of any of the least want of courage or fidelity to Us, or Our service, in that action." The King then formally allowed the seven officers to give their opinions on that point; and they, perhaps not surprisingly, " did unanimously concur with Us."

The document embodying these findings was given that day under the King's sign manual. Rupert had triumphed. Unfortunately neither the King nor the Prince had the sense to let matters rest there. Charles could not forgive Sir Richard Willis, the Governor of his present citadel, for siding so openly with Rupert; for going out of Newark to meet him, for putting him up in his house, and perhaps for other signs of his devotion of which we do not know. He appointed him to a sinecure position, and made Lord Bellasis Governor of Newark in his place. Willis appealed to the Prince for advice, and there followed a most regrettable scene. The King had just come back from church, and was about to dine, when Rupert, Maurice, Gerrard, Willis himself and about twenty others stormed into the room. Rupert was leading, and he made no obeisance or sign of courtesy to the King. The King ordered the dinner to be taken away, and walked to a corner, whither Rupert, Gerrard and Willis followed him. Willis asked, quite respectfully, who had accused him, saying that his disgrace was common talk; Gerrard said that Digby was a traitor, and that he could prove him so; Rupert burst out three or four times with tirades against Digby, using no respect whatever to the King. At one moment the King gave a heavy sigh, saying " O Nephew! " and later when Rupert again said that Digby was the man who had caused all the trouble between them, the King burst out: " They are all rogues and rascals that say so, and in effect traitors, that seek to dishonour my best subjects! " The King ordered them all to leave the room, except Willis, whom he would speak to alone; but Willis, completely forgetting himself, said that he wanted public satisfaction for a public injury. The officers bowed and left the room; Rupert left without even bowing.

It was a disgraceful business, which did no credit to any who took part in it, unless possibly to the distracted King. That evening, the incident was already being described by the ugly word " mutiny," and the officers taking part sent a petition to the King, reminding him of their services to him, declaring that the word " mutiny " was a " misconstruction," and asking for a court martial or their passports. The King summoned up his reserves of firmness, and they got their passports.

Next morning the Princes and Lord Gerrard came to take their leave. Gerrard made some sort of apology, but the Princes none; and at ten o'clock they rode off to Belvoir, with two hundred officers behind them, while the King stood and watched them from a window, weeping to see them go.

This miserable affair has been described in detail because it serves to explain so much of the inner history of the war from the Royalist side: the indecision and obstinacy of the King, the hot tempers and sensitive moods with which he had to contend among his officers, the inconsistency with which, however loyal, they had to contend in him, and above all the guilt of Digby. If Digby had been killed while he was in the field earlier in the war, how much happier a brotherhood would the Cavaliers have been!

The Prince's and their party rode to Belvoir, and from there sent an emissary to Parliament asking for passports and a safe conduct overseas on behalf of them all. They offered

in return an undertaking to engage in no hostilities
during their journey. Parliament asked for more details,
and in bringing back this message the emissary, Colonel
Osborne, added some titbits of London gossip. Henrietta
Maria was saying in Paris that Rupert had sold the city
of Bristol in exchange for hard cash. The Princes' young
brother Edward, who had proposed at one time to come
over and join Maurice and Rupert, had turned Roman
Catholic and gone to Rome. There was one other item
of news which must have given satisfaction to the angry
Cavaliers at Belvoir, for it described the discomfiture of
Digby. He had been trounced in battle, and had lost
not only all his letters but his ciphers as well: a com-
mittee of Roundheads was now gleefully engaged in
translating them. Parliament had also captured an old
letter of Rupert's, in which he had advised the King to
treat for peace; and Osborne reported that this circum-
stance was reacting in his favour in the matter of his
present application.

But Parliament tried to exact what the Cavaliers at
Belvoir were not prepared to accord: an undertaking
that they would never again bear arms against the
Parliament. So once again they took to their horses and
rode through hostile England to Woodstock, having one
fight on the way. The King was now again at Oxford,
and one of his first acts was to release Will Legge from
his imprisonment. Legge wrote at once to Rupert, saying
that at the first conversation he had had with the King
after his release Charles had given him a full account
of the scene at Newark. Legge was as frank with Rupert
as he had been with Digby on Rupert's own behalf. He

said that he would to God that the unhappy breach had never been, but that they must now look forward and not back. " Honest Will " made it quite clear that he thought it was Rupert's duty to apologise, and in a second letter said:

I am of opinion you should write to your uncle . . . you ought to do it; and if you offered your service to him yet and submitted yourself to his disposing and advice, many of your friends think it could not be a dishonour, but rather the contrary, seeing he is a king, your uncle, and in effect a parent to you.

Lord Dorset also wrote:

If my prayers can prevail, you shall not have the heart to leave us all in our saddest times; . . . truly you should not abandon your uncle in the disastrous condition his evil stars have placed him. Let your resolution be as generous and great as is your birth and courage.

And Secretary Nicholas added, very humbly and respectfully, his own entreaties. Daily the King's fortunes were growing worse: the North had gone, the West was shrinking fast, Newark, Belvoir, all the strongholds fell one by one; Goring fled to France. At last, thanks to the perseverance of Legge and the others, Rupert agreed to acknowledge his fault. The King sent him a blank paper on which to write out his confession and apology; Rupert signed his name at the bottom and returned it blank, signifying that he would confess to anything of which the King might deem him guilty. The reconciliation was complete.

But now there was nothing left to do. The last formed body of Royalist troops in the field, a mere handful under Jacob Astley, was defeated in Gloucestershire at Stow in the Wold; and the old man, taken and disarmed, made to his captors one of the dry remarks for which he was noted: " You have now done your work and may go to play, unless you will fall out among yourselves." The King had resolved to throw himself on the mercy of the Scots, the race from which he sprang, having received some sort of assurance from a French go-between that they would receive him with honour: he did not suspect but was soon to learn that Scottish honour was at the lowest ebb in all its history. He slipped out of Oxford with only two companions, and made his way north in disguise; Rupert begged to be allowed to accompany him, but the King feared that his massive height would give them all away.

It was in April that the King went away, and a few days later Oxford was invested by Fairfax. The defence was conducted by Sir Thomas Glemham, and the Princes took no great part in it. Negotiations for a surrender opened in May without result, but on the 18th of June Charles signed papers at Newcastle authorising the Governors of all those towns still holding out to make their own terms with their besiegers. On the 24th of that month, Oxford yielded at last.

Considering all things, the Parliament dealt leniently with Rupert and Maurice. They were given permission, along with seventy of their followers, to stay six months in the country, provided they did not come within twenty miles of London. This permission was soon withdrawn on the grounds that they had abused the reservation by going to Oatlands in Surrey; there seems to have been some misunderstanding. They had gone to Oatlands with Fairfax's permission to receive a visit from their eldest brother Charles-Louis, who had been living comfortably in London throughout the Civil War, drawing a fat pension from the Parliament, and deploring to all and sundry the worthier part played by his brothers in his uncle's quarrel. It is doubtful if they wanted to see Charles-Louis, but it was important that he should see them: for he had hopes of making his peace with the Emperor, and the Emperor wished to be reassured that the younger brothers would be bound by the undertakings of the eldest. Possibly, on their side, they hoped for money from him, for they were almost penniless themselves, and their train of seventy persons required some maintenance. It included a secretary, three chaplains, nine gentlemen, a steward, two engineers (who had come to England with Rupert originally), an apothecary, two grooms of the chamber, footmen, grooms, a gunsmith, a tailor, and a couple of washerwomen.

Their six months' grace having been cancelled by Parliament, they travelled to Dover by Guildford, Reigate and Maidstone. The last time Rupert had been in Dover was four and a half years earlier, when Charles had sent him back to Holland in hopes that peace might yet be preserved. Now all was lost; and as Rupert made his way to St. Germain, near Paris, and Maurice to The Hague, the fortunes of the House of Stuart seemed very low indeed.

* 6 *

The Fifteen Years of Wandering

IF RUPERT expected a chilly welcome from Henrietta Maria in Paris, he must have been agreeably surprised. A generous letter from the King had preceded him, which reads like an echo of the letter written to the Court of England by his mother long before. " Albeit his passions may sometimes make him mistake, yet I am confident of his honest constancy and courage, having at the last behaved himself very well." The French Court also made much of him. Louis XIV was still a minor, being only eight years old, and affairs were in the hands of the Queen Mother, Anne of Austria, and Cardinal Mazarin, who warmly pressed Rupert to take service under the French Crown. This the punctilious Rupert would only do with the consent of Charles: as soon as that arrived, he was made a Marshal and given command of all the English in France. He at once sent out circular letters to the exiles, inviting them to join him. Fourteen hundred did so, but one application, that of his old adversary Goring, he had no hesitation in refusing. Goring then joined the Spaniards and the following summer, during a campaign in Flanders, Rupert had the satisfaction of defeating his regiment in the field, and the still more exquisite satisfaction of finding that all the prisoners he took, many of them English, promptly enlisted under himself.

The Prince's immediate chief in Flanders was an eccentric and not very competent French Marshal called Gassion, who had a cordial jealousy of his illustrious subordinate. Once at least, when they were surprised in an ambush, Gassion suggested that they should all dismount and then, when Rupert had done so, galloped away with his horse. Rupert managed to extricate himself with a wound in the head, but his campaigning was over for the year. While recovering, he received a friendly letter from Charles, congratulating him on his escape, and saying that all Rupert's actions since their last meeting had more than confirmed Charles's good opinion of him. Charles was now a prisoner in Hampton Court, but no notion of the shameful fate in store for him had as yet entered his mind or anybody else's. No sense of doom hung over the Court at St. Germain, only a pleasurable speculation concerning Rupert's reactions to the impending arrival of Digby.

Rupert knew very well that Henrietta Maria was watching him, determined that the " passions " against which Charles had warned her, and which she herself knew of old, should not break out against Digby. At first he behaved as though butter would not melt in his mouth; and then one morning, before most of the Court was astir, he sent his challenge to Digby, suggesting as a rendezvous a cross-roads in the Forest of Poissy. While Digby was dressing and preparing for the encounter, word of it reached the Queen, who sent Jermyn to order

Digby to consider himself confined to his quarters; but Digby, who now for the first time becomes a rather sympathetic character, was so rude to Jermyn that he went off to offer his services as an extra second to Rupert. The duel was about to begin when the Prince of Wales arrived with a posse of the Queen's guards and arrested Rupert and his seconds—two Frenchmen and Digby's old enemy Gerrard. That evening the Queen and the Prince of Wales made both Rupert and Digby appear in front of them, and state publicly the grounds of their quarrel; Rupert behaved with more moderation than usual, and so won the heart of Digby that not only was their reconciliation complete, but Digby shortly after-wards fought a duel with Wilmot and wounded him for speaking ill of Rupert. With this incident Digby, Wilmot and Goring disappear from the story.

The story, indeed, now takes a new turn; for in the summer of 1648 there was a sudden mutiny in the Parliamentary Navy. Some of the dissentient ships sailed to Holland, some remained in the Downs; that part of the Fleet which was in Portsmouth retained its loyalty for the Roundheads.

It was decided that the Prince of Wales, accompanied by Rupert and Maurice, should go over to the Downs in one of the frigates that had come to Holland, in an effort to induce more ships' companies to throw in their lot with the King. The Prince of Wales was there as a figurehead; Rupert was the real spokesman. He had to use all his tact, for it was irritation with the Parliament rather than a belated loyalty to the King which was inspiring unrest in the Navy; and Rupert's tentative suggestion that they should sail to the Isle of Wight and liberate Charles, who had been moved to Carisbrooke, found no favour. Batten, one of the senior captains—the same who had bombarded Henrietta Maria at Bridlington,—was a coward. (Years after the Restoration, Charles the Second was to entertain some friends with a tale of this episode: how, when it looked as though there might be some fighting, Batten was in such a sweat from fear that he tied a cravat under his chin to dry it up. Rupert got it into his head that this was some sort of a signal to the enemy, and swore bloodily: "By God, if things go ill the first thing I will do is shoot him." One does not suppose that this threat made Batten much happier.)

Many of the seamen merely wanted to lie off the Thames and plunder shipping as it went in and out; but at last, with great tact, Rupert prevailed on that part of the Fleet which was with him to sail for Holland. The Parliamentary half of the Navy, under Lord Warwick, set off in pursuit, and the rival Fleets, as they had now become, raced each other for the harbour of Helvoetsluys, the Royal portion having spent some days revictualling off Goeree. The two factions arrived at Helvoetsluys neck-and-neck, but an English captain on the quay refused to take a rope for the leading Parliamentary boat, and made fast Rupert's instead. There followed an absurd few weeks, with the Royal ships in the inner harbour, and the Parliament's in the outer, each trying to woo the crews of the other half from their allegiance. The Dutch, fearing a battle within the harbour, sent a squadron to interpose between the two, warning both that it would treat as hostile whichever should first open fire upon the other. The Prince saw to it that in each of his four ships and five frigates there was a leavening of trustworthy loyalists. Even so, in one of them, the *Antelope*, he only prevented a mutiny by picking up the ringleader in his strong arms and holding him over the side as though to drop him. This is but one of many incidents in his career which show him to have been of more than ordinary strength and stature.

He had moored one of his vessels across the harbour, to prevent Warwick's boats approaching the others, and trained guns down-river to cover the Roundhead ships. Despite all his precautions there was a constant trickle of deserters back to the main fleet before it finally sailed for England on the 21st of November. The Prince was greatly relieved to see it go. He had unfortunately missed, through his preoccupations, the chance of seeing Montrose, who had some plan to propound, and had more than once sent him letters from Brussels suggesting a meeting. " While I am severing the goats from the sheep," wrote Rupert, " I dare not absent myself without hazard." But he had now been officially appointed to the command of the ships, enjoying even the confidence of Hyde, who wrote that in these matters he " hath expressed greater dexterity and temper than you can imagine." One important venture had miscarried: an attempt at rescuing the King from the Isle of Wight. Charles himself had proposed it, sending over Will Legge to Rupert with the plan in his head, for it was too secret to commit to paper. Rupert's own ships being all bottled up at Helvoetsluys, he had borrowed and sent a Dutch vessel for the purpose, which backed and filled for several days off the Isle, persuading a Roundhead ship which came to search her that she was merely awaiting a fair wind. But Charles was unable to reach the rendezvous, and the ship had to return without him.

Want of money made it difficult to equip and victual the little squadron, but it was achieved at last by various means. Rupert's mother pawned her jewels; little Lord Craven once again subscribed handsomely; two prizes were taken, and the proceeds added to the fund; the *Antelope's* guns were sold. Even so, all the ships were sadly undermanned when they sailed on the 21st of January, 1649, in company with three Dutch vessels bound for the Indies. These three extra sail made the squadron appear more formidable than in fact it was; they sailed right through a Parliamentary squadron lying near the Downs without interference, and bore away past the Downs without enemy let or hindrance, down Channel to Kinsale in Ireland, where Ormond, the King's Lord Lieutenant, was awaiting them. Here in a short time they heard rumours, followed by horrible confirmation, that the King had been beheaded in London on the 30th of January.

There is no need to describe in detail the events leading up to the death of the King. Jacob Astley's prediction, that the victors of the Civil War might fall out among themselves, had come true; and the defection of the very ships which Rupert was now commanding had been one of the results of the split. One faction was beginning to wonder whether a monarchy, under proper safeguards, was not the best form of government after all; they had developed, too late, the same conception as had been apparent in Fairfax's summons to Rupert from the lines outside Bristol. Yet Fairfax himself was engaged with Cromwell in putting down the insurrection; and concerning the King Cromwell had said darkly: " We will cut off his head with the crown upon it."

Now the " horrid wickedness," as Hyde called it in a letter to Rupert at Kinsale, was done; " it is no wonder we were all struck into that amazement with the deadly news of it, that we have not yet recovered our spirits to think or do as we ought. That it should be done in the light of the sun, and in that manner, I think no man could imagine . . . I hope it will put new fire of honest rage and fury into us." To the service of the new King, from whom he at once received a fresh Commission confirming him in his command of the ships, Rupert pledged himself completely. He was able to run supplies into the Isles of Scilly, which still held out for the King, and many of whose inhabitants to-day still trace their descent from that last defiant garrison—Bamfields, Mumfords, Hickses, Jenkinses. But soon a strong Parliamentary squadron under Blake—who, like Rupert himself, was a soldier newly turned sailor—blockaded him in Kinsale, where he was obliged to spend the whole of the summer. Sooner or later, he knew, the autumn or winter gales must force Blake to relax his watch upon the harbour. As early as July it was known in the Parliamentary fleet that he was concentrating all his efforts on equipping " his five best sailers " at the expense of the others: they deduced correctly that he was hoping to slip out as soon as a chance offered. Blake defied and rode out the westerly gales of the equinox, being under the lee of the coast of Ireland; but in November the weather went easterly, and although he tried to maintain his station by constant beating to windward a few miles out to sea, his ships were soon scattered.

Rupert seized his chance, and turning the north-easterly wind to good account sailed for Portugal. His ships were scattered in the Bay of Biscay, while hove-to in bad weather, but Rupert had given the Berlinga Islands, on the coast of Portugal, as rendezvous, and all the squadron reached it. By the time they arrived in the Tagus, they had made four prizes, two of which had fallen to Maurice. The King of Portugal welcomed them warmly, and made them free of Oeiras Bay, far up the estuary, promising his protection; the guns of his forts saluted them as they sailed in. While the cargoes of the prizes, all English vessels, were being sold to Portuguese merchants—they realised £40,000—and the prizes themselves being converted into men-of-war, the two Princes were being royally entertained at the King's court.

As soon as the Parliament knew for certain that Rupert had escaped from Kinsale, Blake was ordered to take ten ships and to pursue Rupert wherever he had gone. Blake soon fell in with a ship from Cadiz, which confirmed that Rupert had been seen in Spanish waters. On the 10th of March, just as Rupert was preparing to leave the Tagus, Blake's squadron dropped anchor at its mouth, and sent an envoy ashore requiring the King of Portugal either to deliver up the Princes, or to force them to put to sea forthwith. The young King was so incensed at this demand that he toyed quite seriously with the idea of boarding Rupert's ship for what looked like a promising battle; but he was finally content to ask Blake to give the Princes a clear run of three days without pursuit. Blake refused, and another blockade began, similar to those of Helvoetsluys and Kinsale. Rupert spent much of his time hunting and became a well-known and popular figure among the local people.

A heavy gale soon after Blake's arrival had driven him farther up the estuary, to a new anchorage only two miles from Rupert's. The King required him to give an undertaking not to fight Rupert without the King's written permission. But once again, as with Warwick's men in Holland, there were brawls ashore between the men of the rival Fleets. Blake hatched a plot to kidnap Rupert while he was out hunting, which nearly succeeded; Rupert in return tried to put a home-made time-bomb aboard one of Blake's ships, by disguising one of his men as a Portuguese pedlar in a boat, but the man gave himself away by swearing in English. There was another odd incident when two French men-of-war came into the Tagus to see Rupert, and anchored among Blake's squadron by mistake, despite several signal guns fired by Rupert to warn them. Blake released them when the King of Portugal told him that he would regard their detention as an act of war; and the chief interest lies in a curious sequel, years later, which will be narrated in its due place.

The King of Portugal was strongly in favour of Rupert, and was still able to keep in check those of his advisers who, with an eye to their country's mercantile interests,

wished to back the English Parliament and to enjoy the
fruits of English trade. He now told Blake that he had
abused the hospitality of the Tagus, and could no longer
stay in its harbours. Blake took his revenge on the 16th
of May, by intercepting a convoy bound for Brazil, and
making prizes of nine English ships in it which were
sailing with Portuguese freights. The anti-Rupert party
at Lisbon gained considerable ground, and the King was
glad enough at the prospect of getting rid of his embarras-
sing guest without loss of honour when Rupert tried to
sail on the 27th of July. Portuguese men-of-war were
ordered to escort him past Blake, but the attempt was
abortive; so was another in September, when Rupert
tried to slip through in a fog, lost touch with his own
ships, and had his foretopmast shot down by the Parliamentary squadron. A week later Blake intercepted an
incoming Portuguese convoy from Brazil, and by now
the clamour in Lisbon was stronger than the King could
resist: both he and Rupert were in a dilemma, from
which they were only rescued by the equinoctial gales.
Blake was once more forced away from his blockading
station, and Rupert got out of the Tagus with six ships,
and clear away to sea. The King of Portugal had acted
as a man of honour, but he begged Rupert not to embroil
him any more either with the government of England
or his own people; and the keeper of Rupert's log wrote
that from then on " new misfortunes being no novelty to
us, we plough the sea for a subsistence, and being destitute
of a port we take the confines of the Mediterranean Sea
for our harbour; poverty and despair being companions,
and revenge our guide."

He might almost have added:—" and piracy our profession," for it was little else. They took two prizes before passing through the Straits of Gibraltar; they tried to seize more in Malaga, but were foiled by some of their own men deserting in a small boat and giving the alarm; they tried again to seize some English ships in Velez-Malaga, but the Spaniards burned them before they could get them; they chased three more English ships ashore farther along the coast. They cruised for some days off Cartagena, falling in with one of their own number, from which they had been separated (she had picked up a prize meanwhile); they chased another English ship bound from Archangel to Leghorn, from the coast of Spain almost to Tunis, and took her also. Some of the squadron were now caught by Blake's ships off Cartagena; they sought refuge in the harbour, but the Spaniards, not surprisingly, refused them protection: two of the ships were burnt by the crews, and a third was surrendered to the Parliament through the treachery of the seamen. Rupert and Maurice were still in company, and bound for Toulon; they were separated by a heavy gale, but eventually forgathered there.

At Toulon the prizes were converted into money, and Rupert set about reorganising his squadron. He managed to spread abroad reports that he was bound for the Levant, and Popham, who had been left by Blake to shadow him, set off in that direction, although with some misgiving. When at last the Royal squadron left Toulon, it consisted of five sail: the *Constant Reformation* (Rupert), the *Swallow* (Maurice), the *Honest Seaman* (newly bought with prize-money), the *Loyal Subject* (belonging to an

English captain, whom they had met at Toulon, and who elected to join them), and the best of the prizes, which they christened the *Revenge*. It would be tedious to retail their adventures in detail, but they sailed first by the Algerian coast and so through the Straits to the Canaries, Madeira and the Azores, where they victualled. There was a good deal of trouble with the crews, and the fact that Rupert wanted to make for the West Indies made them discontented and insolent.

Nevertheless they were at heart devoted to the Prince, as they were soon to show. It was found on the way to the Azores that the *Constant Reformation* was making water badly, and her hold was so fully stowed with prize-cargo that they could not discover the leak. Bad weather drove them to sea earlier than they intended to sail, and the leak got worse and worse until soon it was gaining fast upon the pumps. The weather deteriorated; both the *Reformation* and the *Swallow* lost their boats, which were towing astern; and now the *Reformation* was in a very bad way. Early on the third day a huge gap yawned in her hull. They stuffed it with beef and wood, but these measures failed to staunch the leak; they jettisoned their guns to lighten the ship, and cut away the mainmast, but it was obvious that she was foundering. Maurice in the *Swallow* ran up under her stern and the *Honest Seaman* on her weather bow, but they could do nothing to help. And then these men, who had been on the verge of mutiny a few days before, resolved suddenly that whatever happened to them they would save their Prince; they behaved, as the diarist put it, " like souls of a new stamp." One small boat, hoisted inboard, still survived, and the men proposed that they should use it to transfer Rupert to another vessel. The Prince indignantly refused to leave them, but " his men, seeing supplications would not prevail, having selected a crew of undaunted lads, hoisted out their boat and by force put him into it, desiring him at parting to remember they died his true servants." They put him aboard the *Honest Seaman*, the nearest ship, and went back for another boatload, which they brought, and the small boat then sank. The Prince tried to work his new vessel alongside his old, but the force of the gale was such that every time he got near her his own ship fell off. The crew of the *Constant Reformation* were seen to partake of Holy Communion, and after dark to burn two torches; that was the last seen of them. Three hundred and thirty-three men went down with her, and among them was Mortaigne, a Frenchman who had shared with Rupert all the adventures of the Civil War, of the siege of Bristol and the campaign in Flanders.

Next day, Rupert, desperately unhappy and moved at the manner of his deliverance, was rowed across in better weather to Maurice's ship. His troubles were far from over. With his comrades in the *Constant Reformation* had also gone most of the treasure and merchandise captured hitherto. A few days later the *Loyal Subject* dragged her anchors in another gale, went ashore, and became a total loss. The Captain and Master of the *Swallow* led a new dissension; they wanted to go and prey on the shipping in the English Channel rather than continue to cruise in blue water. At last they sailed for Cape Blanco on the coast of Africa, just south of what is now the Spanish colony of Rio de Oro. Landing to victual among the negroes, they found that they all ran away, except for one tiny boy, too small to run. The natives remained hostile, and Rupert kept the boy, who served him for many years as a blackamoor page. Next, by way of the Cape Verde Islands, they sailed to Gambia, where they took as prizes four English ships which they found trading in the river; Maurice took the biggest of them, the *Defiance*, to be his flagship.

The Prince was now resolved to make for the West Indies, where he had hopes of finding islands still loyal to the Crown, in which he might make his base and from which he might capture Parliamentary shipping. Not only was his ability to victual his ships and pay his crews dependent on his successful piracy: his squadron was also the only source of revenue for the exiled Court at St. Germain, to which he had sent substantial remittances from both Lisbon and Toulon. The first stage of the voyage was to the Cape Verde Islands, where one of the ships, the *Revenge*, left the squadron; her captain, says the Prince's log, had been " too covetous of new men," and had filled up his ship's complement with a high proportion of seamen taken from prizes, who seized the ship and sailed for England. The surviving ships of the squadron had an anxious voyage across the Atlantic; they were all in need of refitting, and all leaking, and it was a great relief to bring up at last in a secluded bay of St. Lucia in the Windward Islands. Here all was put to rights; the men had a run ashore, feasted on wild boar and delicious tropical fruits, and restored their spirits.

The next island to the northward is Martinique, belonging to the French; and here they were well received and entertained, but learned to their dismay that all the English islands were now in the possession of the Parliament. None the less, they worked their way north taking a few prizes and dismaying the local garrisons, until a hurricane dealt them the greatest blow of all. It caught them in the rocky passage between the Virgin and Leeward Islands. For two days they were driven before the wind, unable to see or to work the ships; and when at last it abated the *Honest Seaman* was a total wreck on the coast of Porto Rico, and Maurice's *Defiance* had disappeared for ever.

Rupert was not to be consoled for the loss of his brother, who, for all his faults, had been brave and constant; had never queried a decision; and had followed him with devotion and stood by him in every scrape since the days when they had been mischievous boys at Leyden. The blow would have been easier to bear if his fate had been certainly known; Rupert could not be sure that the black Caribbean gale which had swallowed him up might not have cast him ashore somewhere, without his ship, but safe. For many years there were rumours that Maurice was a prisoner in Spanish hands, or pulling an oar in a Spanish galley. In the middle fifties there was a tale that he was a slave in Algeria. Sir Richard Fanshaw, Ambassador in Spain in 1663, gathered various statements from Englishmen and others of a mysterious person of quality who had been lying a prisoner in Porto Rico jail five years before. In the same year one Fedric de Schamps wrote to Rupert saying that he had made inquiries in Tortuga, an island off Venezuela, five hundred miles due south of where the *Defiance* was last seen; he had no doubt that Maurice was then dead, though there were some grounds for belief that he had got ashore alive. Nothing definite was ever heard.

With a heavy heart Rupert sailed for home in his only remaining ship, the *Swallow*, provisioning himself from a few last-minute prizes and the French hospitality of Guadeloupe. He had hoped to replenish in the Azores, but for some reason he was received with hostility instead of hospitality as before. By the time he made his landfall off the mouth of the Loire his crew was on short rations. Ill luck pursued them to the end of their voyage, for the *Swallow* went aground while under the pilot as she sailed up river; and some months later, while being refitted, she caught fire and was burnt out.

There are those who say that this three years' voyage of Rupert was a buccaneering venture, pure and simple, and that even if it did not start as such it ended as little better. The defence will urge that he made little or no personal profit; that all he made went to the King, as his chief, if not his only, source of revenue; and that Rupert's true achievement was to maintain the honour of the Crown of England by showing its flag, afloat but still embattled, after it had been driven from English shores. Whatever the truth, it was no mean feat to have kept the seas for three long years, with little encouragement, no base, leaky ships and near-mutinous crews.

He received at first a tumultuous welcome, from the King, the Queen Mother, all the courtiers and the French

Court as well; but they noticed that hardship and
sorrow had greatly changed him. He was far from fit
and subject to long bouts of moroseness; the atmosphere
about him was charged with mystery, and old Roundhead
stories were recalled about his dabblings in black arts.
He had brought back curious drugs from Guinea and
the Indies; his blackamoor page was always with him.
Soon there was trouble about the disposal of his treasure
and the payment of the bills which he had incurred
two years before at Toulon. Charles was induced to ask
him for exact accounts of the proceeds of the voyage,
which he took as an insult. To have his honesty called
into question, after all he had endured while the rest of
the exiles were living in comparative though impoverished
comfort at St. Germain, would have been intolerable to
a less fiery temper than his. But for his efforts there
would have been no money at all. The same wrangles
about policy, with everyone engaged in constant intrigues,
were still going on as though Rupert had never been
away. He lent his support to one discreditable affair,
the attempted assassination of Cromwell by a man called
Henshaw; the Parliamentary ambassadors to Holland
and Spain had both been murdered by Royalist agents
during his absence at sea. But when, after some disagreement with Rupert and others, Charles blurted out that
they should " never more have his trust or his company,"
Rupert decided that he had had more than he could
stomach, and left the Court for Germany, despite Charles's
repentance and belated assurance of love and friendship.

Rupert's wanderings of the next few years are of little
interest. His brother Charles-Louis had recovered his

Electorate and Rupert, who was toying with the idea
of settling down there, spent some time with him at
Heidelberg until they too quarrelled. Rupert then swore
that he would never return, and stuck to this resolution
even when, years afterwards, Charles-Louis begged him to
come home. Although away from St. Germain, Rupert
had already returned to the one service from which all
the affronts in the world could never succeed in finally
estranging him; and he had raised a loan for Charles
from private persons in the Palatinate after Charles-Louis
had refused one. He stayed also with the Emperor, by
whom he was well received; the friends whom he had
made during his imprisonment nearly twenty years before
still remembered him with affection as well as regret;
and he not only raised another loan for Charles, but
recovered for himself from the Emperor a fair sum to
which he had become entitled under a treaty concluded
in his absence. In 1657 he is reported as being in the
service of the King of Hungary, " who they say will owe
his Empirate to his sword." The two years immediately
before the Restoration of Charles the Second he appears
to have spent quietly in Mainz, working at chemistry,
which always fascinated him, and in drawing; here he
perfected the process of the mezzotint, of which he was
probably the inventor, and which he was later to introduce
into England. He had spent his savings and was living in
comparative poverty, when the news came of the over-
throw of Parliament and the new regime in England.

* 7 *

Harvest

O<small>N THE</small> 25th of May 1660 Charles the Second landed
at Dover; four days later he was in London.
Monk, who had been the mouthpiece and the prime
mover of those responsible for the King's return, had
served the Parliament for a good many years; but before
that he had fought for the Crown under Ormond in
Ireland, and again until taken prisoner in 1644 at
Nantwich. Fairfax, who had quarrelled with Cromwell
soon after the execution of Charles the First, was also
among those who had enabled the King to come back
to his own again. But the rejoicings of the first days
of the new reign were mingled with reprisals: a dozen
regicides were hanged, drawn and quartered within sight
of the spot where they had killed the old King, while
the bodies of Cromwell and others who had died before
vengeance could overtake them were disinterred and
hung up at Tyburn. Fairfax withdrew into private life;
Monk became Duke of Albemarle, and took his place
among such returning exiles as Ormond and Secretary
Nicholas on the new Privy Council. Hyde became its
President.

Neither gratitude nor a sense of what was fitting were

prominent among Charles's virtues; but he lost no time in inviting his cousin Rupert to join him and to share in his recovered prosperity. Rupert was sick at the time from one of his tropical fevers, but he arrived in London at the end of September, and Pepys wrote in his diary: " Prince Rupert is come to the Court, welcome to nobody."

Why Pepys should have said this so soon one cannot tell, for the warmth and gratitude with which the Prince was generally received was all that he could have wished. Of two hundred and seventeen pensions which Charles immediately granted to those who had served his family faithfully, amounting to nearly £80,000 a year, Rupert's £6,000 was among the most generous. A few months of England were so much to his taste that he resolved to make his home there. His mother had made the same decision; she settled down in a house of Craven's, where she died in February 1662. Rupert had had a happy reunion with his old comrade Will Legge, who had spent the last nine years in prison, and he made him his agent when he went abroad in 1661 to take his final farewell of the Continent, and his official leave from the Emperor, in whose service he technically was. He was nothing if not punctilious: his old Commission as President of Wales was still in force, having not been included when Charles the First stripped him of all military authority after the disaster at Bristol; but he resigned it, saying that he would not hold commissions from any source but the new King.

He returned to England, having discharged his duty in Germany, early in 1662 just in time to see his mother before she died. He quickly engaged in the public service. As was to be expected, he took a great interest in the Navy; any merchant venture oversea was sure of his eager support, if not interference; he was one of the founder members of the Royal Society; and he was appointed to the Board set up to administer Tangier, which had come to Charles as part of his dowry on his marriage to Catherine of Braganza. Poor Pepys, who hated Rupert like poison—and Rupert had no use for him—was also on the Tangier Board; he noted one day in his diary:

A sad consideration to see things of so great weight managed in so confused a manner as it is; Prince Rupert do nothing but swear and laugh a little, with an oathe or two, and that's all he do.

But Rupert had introduced into England one parlour trick of his own invention which Pepys admired, the little glass droplets which resist all attempts to break them until they are struck at the tapering end, when they shatter: they are still called " Prince Rupert's drops," but to Pepys they were " the chymicall glasses . . . a great mystery to me."

In 1664 the rover in him came out again, and he took command of a squadron which it was proposed to send against the Dutch in Guinea. He was in high spirits when he set off, hoping to bring back quantities of treasure, and excited about two scientific commissions with which the Royal Society had entrusted him—testing out a new sounding device without the use of a line, and dredging up samples of water from the bottom of the sea. Pepys had overheard him in Monk's house saying boisterously: " God damn me, I can answer but for one ship, and in that I will do my part, for it is not as in an army where a man can command everything." The King, the Duke of York and half the Court saw him go on board his flagship *Henrietta* at three o'clock in the morning in London River, after a supper-party; but he got no farther than Portsmouth. There was a threat of war nearer home; and he himself fell seriously ill, owing, said his friends, to an outbreak of the wound in his head suffered in Flanders in 1648, when Gassion abandoned him; his enemies ascribed his malady to recent dissolute living. The expedition was abandoned, and Rupert carried to London, where he slowly recovered his health.

The Dutch War broke out in March 1665. The prime cause was colonial rivalry; the Dutch were trying to deny to English ships the right to trade in seas which they regarded as their sphere of influence and commerce. Three squadrons under the Duke of York, Rupert and Lord Sandwich sailed for Holland in April, hoping to intercept returning convoys; they spent a fortnight off the Texel, and were then obliged to return to Harwich for want of provisions. Want of provisions and lack of equipment run like a refrain through all the correspondence between Rupert and the Admiralty, and Pepys is for ever wringing his hands at Rupert's written thunderbolts.

On the 3rd of June was fought the battle of Solebay (Southwold Bay). Over a hundred ships were engaged on either side, the English being slightly the stronger; Rupert led the van with the Duke of York next and Sandwich last, and the English had the best of the encounter; but the pursuit was broken off owing to one of the Duke of York's gentlemen producing false orders while his master was asleep. There was some unprofitable squabbling after the battle about the respective parts played by Sandwich and Rupert, in which Sandwich complained that Rupert got more credit than he, although Rupert's section of the Fleet had suffered less damage and no casualties. And some friends of Rupert's in Parliament moved that the House should vote him £10,000 and Sandwich half a crown.

For a short time Rupert was out of employment, but in 1666 he was given joint command of the Fleet with Monk, with whom he got on extremely well. They had known each other at Breda nearly thirty years before; and although they had not met during the Civil War, Rupert had made efforts to make an exchange for Monk after his capture at Nantwich. Like Rupert, Monk had considerable fighting experience by sea as well as by land; he had taken part many years before in an expedition against Cadiz, and had fought the Dutch at sea during the years of the Commonwealth. In spite of this, Monk was tactful enough, to " declare modestly upon all occasions that he was no seaman." At all events, they tackled the job which confronted them in a scientific manner, pooling their experience of naval tactics in general and Dutch naval tactics in particular.

The result was their famous " Fighting Instructions " which are admitted by all authorities to have anticipated by a century the classic teachings of Nelson. Shorn of technicalities, their purpose was to ensure that an enemy, no matter how unwilling, could be brought to action, regardless of the rigid conventions in force in those days, which so easily became the admiral's master rather than his servant. They enshrined the principle that " line or no line, signals or no signals, the destruction of the enemy is always to be the chiefest care."

Their first battle as joint admirals did not work out as they had hoped and planned. Monk and he sailed together from the Nore on the 23rd of May; but owing to a rumour that French ships were coming up Channel to join the main Dutch fleet—for France was now allied with Holland—Rupert was sent westward with a third of the available ships to intercept. The wind was easterly and he was therefore far away to leeward when Monk encountered the Dutch in the Downs, engaged them, and thus started the Four Days' Battle. Despite his inferior numbers—the Dutch had eighty-five ships to his fifty-six—Monk fought them successfully, the battle drifting across the mouth of the Thames estuary towards the north-east, until Rupert could beat back up Channel and join forces on the afternoon of the third day. The Dutch then allowed the English to disengage, which Monk and Rupert did by means of a manœuvre which they had just worked out, covering the disabled ships with those least injured.

Rupert was asked in the following year to furnish a report for the House of Commons to explain why the Dutch had had the best of the action. He began by saying how happy he was that his own services had found favour, and then proceeded to give a robust answer, observing that if Monk's orders had been strictly obeyed, as they should have been, the victory would have been greater. His five reasons were: Faulty intelligence; " intolerable neglect in supplying provisions during the whole summer's expedition, notwithstanding the extraordinary and frequent importunity of our letters "; want of seamen, who preferred to serve in merchant ships and colliers, for better pay and less hazard; the " horrible neglect of His Majesty's officers and the workmen of his yards "; and dispersal of the Fleet.

In July, they put to sea again and met the Dutch near the Galloper Shoal off the North Foreland. This time the new tactics met with a triumphant success. The Dutch lost twenty ships out of a hundred and thirty engaged against the English loss of one, and withdrew to Holland. A fortnight later Rupert arrived off their coast with a squadron, and carried out one of the most destructive raids in history. He sent one ship, the *Pembroke*, with a great many small boats, through a shallow channel leading behind the island of Vlieland. The raiding party was commanded by Sir Robert Holmes, who had long ago been Maurice's page, and who had followed Rupert through the Civil War, Flanders and the West Indies. He burned something like a hundred richly laden merchantmen from the Indies, Guinea, the Spice Islands and the Baltic, and got away again in bad weather, with only a foot of water under the *Pembroke's* keel. " Of a goodly number of shipping which were there proudly riding about one of the clock, there remained nothing but so many consuming keels at eight in the evening." No wonder that this exploit became known in England as "Sir Robert Holmes's bonfire."

Back on the English coast, they awaited reprisals; but these did not come until June of the following year. Most of the English ships were out of commission for reasons of economy, when De Ruyter sailed boldly in and burned them in the Medway. Meanwhile one of Rupert's ships had snapped up a French one which had mistaken Rupert's for a Dutchman; and her captain was none other than the man who had made the same mistake fifteen years before, and had gone alongside Blake in the Tagus in mistake for Rupert.[1]

As the summer came to an end and the Fleet laid up for the winter, Rupert launched a tirade against those responsible for provisioning. Pepys and his colleagues were haled before the King, the Duke of York, Rupert, Hyde and various others, and asked to account for their failure to keep the Fleet supplied. According to his own diary, Pepys made what he himself reckoned to be a good speech, pointing out how much there was to be done with how little money; and Rupert lost his temper, "rising up in a great heat." Pepys had his figures at his fingertips, while Rupert, for all the passion for statistics with which he was later credited, had not. The Secretary of the Navy won his point, but he went home an apprehensive man. Batten was sent down to report on the state of the Fleet; but when he returned to give the Council an account of his inspection he was so dismayed by the presence there of his old adversary Rupert, which he had not expected, that he made a poor showing. He

[1]See page 111.

confessed afterwards to Pepys that "he knew the Prince too well to anger him, and was afraid to do it." The Prince was thus able to let himself go in the report to the House of Commons already mentioned.

Rupert was still not at all well, suffering from the old wound in his head. Some splinter was pressing on his skull, and he had to undergo a trepanning operation. He went to recuperate in November at Tunbridge Wells, where the Court had also gone. There he met and fell in love with a pretty young actress, Peg Hughes, to the amusement of Charles and the Court, for he was more than old enough to be her father. For some time she resisted his approaches, but at last became his mistress; he established her in a house at Hammersmith, and for the rest of his life they remained happy in each other's company. By her he had a daughter, Ruperta, who inherited her mother's looks, and eventually married a general; her descendants are living yet.

It was at this time that he was painted by Lely, which in Pepys's estimation was "very finely done indeed." In the following year, 1668, he was appointed to the Governorship of Windsor, a post of which he was proud in a place which he adored. He loved showing people round it; Evelyn the diarist describes how Rupert showed him all the improvements which he had been making and all the swords and accoutrements from the earliest times with which he had been decorating the walls. He entertained the Prince of Orange there one Christmas; and in a contemporary letter we read:

The King and Duke go next week to Windsor for

another hunting bout, the Prince endeavouring to make them as much in love with that place as he can, who is building, fortifying and making many additions in the Castle.

He built there also in a separate house a laboratory with every sort of apparatus for his chemical experiments, and fitted up a turret of the Castle in the same way. One evening, when he had been some years established at Windsor, the King and the Duke of York were there with a large number of courtiers. The Royalties had gone to bed, but the courtiers were still revelling. Soon they had " drunke away all reason; at last they began to despise art too, and brake into Prince Rupert's Laboratory, and dashed his stills and other chymicall instruments in pieces." Nor did the brawling end there, for they soon began to quarrel among themselves, and one of them stabbed another. At three in the morning the Duke of York woke up the King and asked him if he proposed to lie in bed and have his throat cut. The King got up and dressed at once, and both of them went back there and then to Whitehall.

For all his love of it, Windsor seems to have been a dangerous place in those days. One summer evening there was another dispute between Peg Hughes's brother, who was in Rupert's employment, and one of the King's servants, as to whether Peg Hughes or Nell Gwynn, both of whom were staying there, was the prettier woman. They came to blows and Hughes was killed. Rupert's reaction to this affair is not on record, but he had never been averse from duelling himself, and perhaps he thought it was all in order.

The wanton wrecking of his laboratory, however, must have annoyed him considerably, for he took his scientific and artistic work very seriously. He took out a patent in July 1671 for work which he had been doing at Windsor on " iron cannon, to do the same execution as brass or steel," and Pepys made a note, undated, to say that he had had a very good account of Prince Rupert's invention of " great guns." Later on Pepys believes he has unearthed a scandal: for somebody tells him that the guns are no better than the old ones; that the Treasury is paying for them at the rate of £60 a ton, whereas the royal founders have offered to cast them at a third of the price; and that the profits are going to three partners, Lord Shaftesbury, the Prince and the Master of the Ordnance. He ends his note: " Quaere: More particulars about this matter."

Other experiments which he made at Windsor concerned a new method of tempering gun-barrels in a " glasshouse," and a new method of boring them by hydraulic power. He invented a kind of revolver, experimented with the idea of a torpedo, made a new kind of lock for firearms, developed a new and very much more powerful formula for gunpowder, devised a new form of shot, and produced refinements for various nautical instruments. He amused himself also with his mezzotinting; several of his mezzotints are still at Windsor, and beautiful work they are. Another side-line was experimenting with dies, and he must have astonished and disconcerted the Master of the Mint by his forging of coins. He had somehow got hold of a broken die which had been used for making farthings, and patched it up. The result was surprisingly good. "Really it is rarely well done," wrote somebody to the Master of the Mint," and saving that it is not so deep as the original it would puzzle yourself the Master to say it were a counterfeit, and this fault too the Prince says he can remedy. He commanded me to send you this piece." Such was his reputation for ingenuity that when, two or three years before his death, some French cipher message fell into English hands which nobody could interpret, it was sent to him in hope that he might break it where others had failed; but he too was defeated, although he claimed to have made out the words: "Strike, strike, strike."

He was out of doors as much as in, either shooting or hunting. He had his own pack of hounds under his huntsman, Tayler; and he rode about Berkshire, of which he was now Lord Lieutenant, as eagerly as in the days when he rode from Maidenhead to Windsor at the head of his cavalry. But now, instead of being their terror, he was a familiar and popular figure among the country people.

Not all this time was spent at Windsor. He never again set foot on the Continent, although he had a house at Rhenen in Germany which he used to lend to the Duke of Monmouth and others; but he lived a good deal in London, where his house was in Spring Gardens, close to where Pall Mall runs into Trafalgar Square. Here he was handy both for work and recreation. He played tennis regularly at St. James's, and was said to

be one of the four best players in the Kingdom. Despite
Pepys's remarks about his conduct at the meetings of the
Tangier Board, he took his work seriously; and when
in 1673 the Test Act was passed, which debarred the
Duke of York as a Catholic from continuing in the office
of Lord High Admiral, Rupert was one of the twelve
members of the Board which took over his duties.
Contrary to his reputation, Charles himself was the most
regular attendant at its meetings; Rupert's record of
attendance was better than most, and his absences are
chiefly accounted for by his being away with the Fleet.
The Board at first met three times a week at 8 a.m. and
later twice a week at 8.30. Pepys did not enjoy these
occasions at all. Rupert's age, experience and reputation
enabled him to be irascible with impunity; perhaps he
was becoming a bit of a Colonel Blimp.

In 1672 a third and rather half-hearted war had
broken out against the Dutch. The Duke of York commanded the Fleet at first, but the introduction of the
Test Act debarred him thenceforward, and Rupert took
his place. He fought some inconclusive actions without
great success; but his popularity in the Navy and the
country was now so great that he lost no reputation.
Stories of his hot temper were circulated with delight:
how he threatened the Commissioners of the Navy with
his cane; how the King had "said merrily, the day
before he went to see him, that he [the King] must
expect a chiding;" how he had fired on one of his own
captains for flying a flag to which he was not entitled;
how he had said that he would never thrive at sea until
some had been hanged on land. Once a timorous letter

went to Rupert from the Admiralty saying that, as nothing had been heard from him for some time, it was presumed that he had all he needed; another time a letter came from him saying:

The demands are answered by accounts from Mr. Pepys of what has been sent to the Fleet, which will not satisfy the ships unless the provisions could be found.

Yet when he at last returns ashore, we find somebody writing:

Prince Rupert has come to town from the Fleet, and has been received by the whole Court and Town with the greatest expressions of affection imaginable.

When the war finally ended in 1674, it was agreed that a state of peace should exist from the 20th February. On the 11th, Rupert heard of a Dutch ship, bound for the West Indies, sheltering in a harbour in Shetland; and he immediately despatched a ship to seize her before the time limit should be up. It was his last act in the war, and his final fling at near-buccaneering.

He could still be high-spirited. It is unfortunate that no date is attached to this scandalised entry by Pepys in his minutes at the Admiralty of a conversation which he had with Sir Phineas Pett, of the shipbuilding family:

Sir Phineas Pett tells me that he met Prince Rupert turning into the River through the Narrow Seas with the *Royal Sovereign*; observing thereupon not only the extraordinary quality of that ship for working, but the no less rashness of the Prince in venturing her; who, asking Sir Phineas what he thought Trinity House would say to see the ship so doing, Sir Phineas answered that he believed they would say His Highness was mad. Whereto the Prince replied, " I believe so too." Sir Phineas noting that if the ship had by chance missed stays never so little she must have been lost, and then what would have been said of both ship and pilot?

There could be no more endearing picture of an old sea-dog revelling in a good sail in a fine ship.

For the past ten years he had been deeply interested in developing commercial ventures in Africa and Canada, just as in his youth he had toyed with the idea of developing Madagascar. The Hudson's Bay Company now became his great interest; Rupert River, which runs into James Bay in Canada, and Prince Rupert House, a centre of the fur trade in London to-day, commemorate his pioneering zeal. In 1678 Pepys records that the King was " prevailed withal at the instance of His Highness " to lend a naval vessel to the Company for a year, at the Company's risk. Two years before he had successfully defended on the grounds of their ignorance the masters of two of the Company's ships, who were in trouble for improperly flying the royal flag. He was not averse from using his position at the Admiralty for forwarding his own interests. When his yacht was stolen, he got the Board to build him another. Twice he sent a small ship

to Germany to bring back Rhine wine for his own use
and the King's, taking good care that the Admiralty
remained responsible for the pay of the crew; once he
directed a man-of-war to bring him back some Spanish
onions. Another time he raised Cain because he was
ordered to pay back £1,100 which he had been overpaid
in error, and he continued to storm for three months
until he was allowed to keep it as " a free gift and
bounty." His rate of pay as Admiral, incidentally, was
four pounds a day, or £1,460 a year.

Twice he is recorded as taking Holy Communion by
the Anglican rite to prove his eligibility for his posts
under the Crown. (Twenty-five years earlier, to make
himself *persona grata* with the Scots, he had emphasised
his devotion to the Calvinistic tenets in which he had
been brought up.) Twice at least he had bright ideas
of lasting benefit to the Navy. The first was to make
good shortages of English timber for shipbuilding by
purchasing in Germany; the second was when he
induced the King to allot £1,000 for selecting forty of
the ablest boys in Christ's Hospital for training as pilots
and shipmasters.

He was growing very old, while the honour in which
he was held grew old with him. He had had a hard life,
and wounds in his head and leg, together with old fevers,
were troubling him. But he still intervened from time
to time to press his counsel on the King, who was said
to be considerably in awe of him. It was he who headed
the Petition to Charles in 1679 to dissolve the Cavalier
Parliament which had sat without a break since 1660;
it had been elected in the first flush of Restoration, and

had long since ceased to reflect the moods of the country. And when one of its old members, Mr. Speke of Somerset, was falsely accused of disloyalty, it was the old Prince who stood up and testified what Speke had not liked to mention: that Speke had sent him a thousand crowns for the defence of Bridgwater in the closing stages of the Civil War, and had never asked for them back, nor even got in touch with Rupert since. Instead of losing his head, as seemed possible, Speke found himself at dinner with the Prince.

One of his last letters was written in French to his youngest sister Sophie only two months before he died. It was to tell her that he had arranged for her to draw a thousand pounds a year during her husband's life; and he added that he hoped that this would make it possible for her son to live for some time in England, to learn the language and make himself known to the people, "which is essential." It was that son, then aged twenty-one, who was afterwards to become George the First of England: and if he had only profited by his uncle's advice, he would have been more of an English king and less of a German makeshift.

In September 1680 there were reports that " Prince Rupert's leg grows worse, and 'tis feared it will soon end him." But he lived for two more years, and when at last he died in Spring Gardens on the 29th of November 1682 it was not only from the infection in his leg but from fever and pleurisy as well. All his life he had had a dread of blood-letting, and he concealed the pleurisy until the last minute. He must have been still in harness for his beloved Company when he died, for a search had to be made among his papers for the title deeds to Port Nelson on Hudson's Bay.

He was buried in great state in Westminster Abbey eight days later. The coffin was preceded by many nobles and gentlemen; Lord Craven, now a very old man, was chief mourner, and among those who followed at the end of the procession were his butler, his huntsman, his tennis-player and his gunsmith. That evening, insensitive as ever, the King and the Duke of York went to the theatre.

Epilogue

LORD CRAVEN was the Prince's executor, and he faithfully discharged this last service to the Palatine family. In an iron box in Rupert's house he found 1694 golden guineas, together with a thousand pounds in silver. He disposed of the plate for £2,070, the pack of hounds for £120, the books for £100, the yacht for £46, a hunter for £40, and the four mares out of the coach for £6 10s. each. Nell Gwynn bought "the great pearl necklace"—could it have been the Elector's wedding present to the Winter Queen?—for £4,520, Colonel Oglethorpe the Prince's guns, and Sir James Hayes his shares in the Hudson's Bay Company. For fifty pounds Lord Craven himself bought in, as a memento of his old friend, a book sumptuously bound in gold and enamel. And he settled what was owing to the Gentleman of the Horse, the Secretary, the Proctor or Treasury Solicitor, the Jeweller, the Perriwig-maker, the Apothecary, and the Undertaker.

Ruperta and her mother each received six thousand pounds. Long afterwards Ruperta's husband went as Envoy Extraordinary to the Court of Hanover on behalf of William the Third of England, where her aunt, Sophia, was Electress. Sophia had always been Rupert's favourite sister, and she took his daughter to her heart. If Rupert had married Ruperta's mother (presuming that to do so he had not been forced to repudiate the succession), Ruperta's claim to the English crown would have been better than that of George the First. It is highly appropriate that her direct descendant and representative to-day should be a member of the Royal Household.

Rupert also had a son, born a few years before Ruperta. His mother was Francesca Bard; and it was her father who had tried to intercede with Rupert for the life of the Governor of Bletchingdon in 1644, and whose message miscarried. The boy was known as Dudley Bard, and showed every sign of being a chip of the old block. He was at school at Eton, where his father could keep an eye on him from Windsor; but he itched to study war like his father, and was put under a military tutor at the Tower of London with a view to his becoming a soldier. At Rupert's death he inherited the house at Rhenen and all such money and property as Rupert had abroad, in the Palatinate and the Empire. He went to Germany to claim it, and returned in time to fight his first campaign against the Duke of Monmouth in the rebellion of 1685, commanding the musketeers at the engagement at Norton St. Philip as " Captain Rupert, the Prince's son." The following year, when still under twenty, he was killed in an assault on the walls of Buda-Pest.

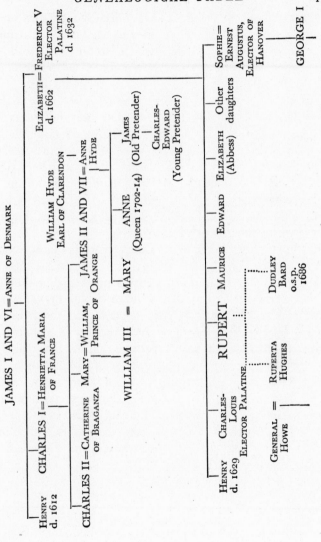

Chronological Table

1619	Born in Prague.
1620	Flight to Holland.
1632	First taste of active service, at Rheinberg.
1636	First visit to England.
1637	Return to Holland. Siege of Breda.
1638 Oct.	Battle of Vlotho; Rupert made prisoner.
1641 Dec.	Freed; return to Holland.
1642 Feb.	Met Charles I at Dover.
1642 Aug.	Joined Charles I in England as General of the Horse.
1642 Sept.	Skirmish at Powicke Bridge.
1642 Oct.	Edgehill.
1643 Sept.	1st Battle of Newbury.
1644 July	Marston Moor.
1644 Oct.	Second Battle of Newbury.
1645 June	Naseby.
1645 Sept.	Surrender of Bristol.
1646	Joined Henrietta Maria at St. Germain.
1648	Service in Flanders.
1649 Jan.	Sailed with squadron from Helvoetsluys; Charles I executed.
1649-52	At Sea.
1652	Return to Nantes.
1653-60	Wanderings on the Continent.
1660 May	Restoration of Charles II.
1660 Sept.	Rupert arrived in London.
1664	Abortive Expedition to Guinea.
1665	Battle of Solebay.
1666	Four Days' Battle. " Sir Robert Holmes's Bonfire."
1668	Appointed Governor of Windsor.
1673	Joined Board of Admiralty.
1682	Died in London.

A Note on Sources

I HAVE already mentioned in the Foreword Eliot Warburton's *Memoirs of Prince Rupert and the Cavaliers*, which includes a mass of correspondence and the Prince's journals. Eva Scott's *Rupert, Prince Palatine* is the only good biography, but it was published in 1899 and has long been out of print. James Cleugh's *Prince Rupert the Cavalier* is the best modern one. I do not care for Miss Margaret Irwin's highly idealised picture in her novel *The Stranger Prince*, which ends in any case with the Civil War.

There are references to Rupert in very many contemporary memoirs, such as those of the Verney family and of Ludlow the Regicide. Clarendon's *History of the Rebellion* reflects its author's lack of enthusiasm for the Prince, but gives an excellent and vivid impression of the time. Rupert's own Journals, kept on his behalf by an unknown writer, are the sole authority for his voyages. Pepys's Manuscripts and Naval Minutes record Rupert's activities and wranglings at the Board of Admiralty. There are no records whatever at Windsor or elsewhere of his long and happy tenure of the Governorship of the Castle.

Colonel A. H. Burne's *The Battlefields of England*, published in 1950, contains many speculations unsupported by evidence, but is the fruit of much industry and an imaginative military mind; and the reconstructions are always feasible.